MARIANNE H. MICKS

Our Search for Identity

Humanity in the Image of God

D0974835

FORTRESS PRESS   PHILADELPHIA

Biblical quotations, unless otherwise noted, are from the Revised Standard Version of the Bible, copyrighted 1946, 1952, © 1971, 1973 by the Division of Christian Education of the National Council of the Churches of Christ in the U.S.A., and are used by permission.

The cartoon captions used on pp. 46–47, are taken from *The New Yorker,* November 4, 1972, May 5, 1973, and February 3, 1973, respectively, and are used by permission from the publisher.

The poetry quotation on p. 100 is taken from *The Collected Poetry of W. H. Auden.* Copyright © 1945 by Random House. Used by permission of the publisher.

The poetry quotation on p. 92 is taken from *Poems,* by C. S. Lewis. Copyright © 1964 by Harcourt Brace Jovanovich. Used by permission of the publisher.

Library of Congress Cataloging in Publication Data

Micks, Marianne H.
 Our search for identity.

 Includes index.
 1. Man (Christian theology) 2. Identification (Religion) 3. Sex (Theology) I. Title.
 BT701.2.M52   233′.5   81–70592
 ISBN 0–8006–1627–8   AACR2

9403K81   Printed in the United States of America   1–1627

In Memory of
Ransom and Robert

Co-workers in Becoming Human

Contents

Preface

As the title of this book suggests, our search for identity is both corporate and continuous. Each new generation takes up the search where its parents left off. It must ask new questions about what it means to be human, because it must take into account ever-expanding horizons and ever-deepening mysteries of life.

Today those new questions confront us almost daily in our newspapers. The "facts" science can offer us to date are too few and too fragile to respond to them conclusively, or even to probe them adequately. Indeed, by the time most of us read about these "facts" in the popular press—much less in book form—they are already outdated. Yet the questions from the natural and behavioral sciences only add to the adventure of our common Christian search for identity, because we do not search for answers only in the columns of the morning newspaper. We are heirs of Scripture and of two thousand years of family history to help us in our search.

The search for identity is also an individual one, and my own search for identity is inevitably revealed in these pages. Like our corporate search, any personal search is also continuous. I do not expect to discover fully who I am until I die. Nevertheless, since I started this study, the deaths of two people I love—my only brother and the friend through whom I was converted to the Christian faith—have increased my understanding of what it means to be human. I dedicate this book to them, with thanksgiving.

I am indebted to many other people for helping me in this work—editors, typists, librarians, writers, colleagues, friends, with all their spouses and children. To them I want to say, "Thank God that you are human, too."

MARIANNE H. MICKS

Virginia Theological Seminary
All Saints Day, 1981

Introduction

Being human is difficult. Becoming human is a lifetime process. True humanity is a gift. Those three convictions color the picture of the Christian doctrine of human being presented in the following chapters. Although they are not uniquely Christian convictions, they are, I think, essential parts of a Christian answer to the question: What does it mean to be human?

What does it mean to be human? That question is older than psychology, sociology, biology, and theology proper. It is the perennial and distinctively human question. Our ability to ask it marks us off as fundamentally different from dogs and cats and dolphins. No one has yet provided a full and final written answer to the question, nor should we expect one. What it means to be human remains a frontier for exploration and discovery. Scientists continue to offer us new knowledge of the territory. So do artists of all kinds—including those creative human beings whom some of us call saints.

Today, Christian understanding of human being is challenged by new thought about the nature of human language, as well as by new social crises. Changing sexual roles demand a reassessment of who we are collectively as creatures of God, maker of all that is, seen and unseen. New recognition of our complex interconnectedness as individuals calls for fresh thinking about human wholeness—about salvation, to use the theological term. Although we have known of our family connections with plants and animals ever since Genesis was written, environmentalists today insist that we must exercise a new humility about the uniqueness of human life in the network of nature.

At the same time, futurists and technologists are raising crucial questions about the durability and the personality of human life in the realm we choose to call history. And again, the explosion of interest in the potentialities of the human spirit—whether it is manifested as interest in glossolalia, yoga, or motorcycle maintenance—evokes yet another look at how human beings are related to Ultimate Reality. One major purpose of this essay, therefore, is to rethink Christian anthropology in dialogue with contemporary thought.

A second major purpose, however, is to remain in active dialogue with biblical and historical anthropology, so that our present understanding of humanity is stretched and deepened by our theological tradition. Most especially, I presuppose that any answers to the questions of being and becoming fully human today are both enriched and judged by the humanity of the one long called "perfect man"—Jesus of Nazareth.

In the perspective of Christian theology, to be human always means to be in relationship. The following explorations (of our relationships with each other, with ourselves, with nature, with history, and with God) do not, therefore, chart new territory in the field of theological anthropology. My intent is rather to help refocus the central questions in that traditional branch of theological inquiry. Granted that we are created in God's image, male and female, what does it mean to be human? To put the question more succinctly: Who are we?

PART I

Social Animals

CHAPTER ONE

The Image
of God

Human life as we know it is ambiguous. The first thing the Bible
says about the human being is also ambiguous. No one is certain
precisely what the writers of the first chapter of Genesis meant
when they said:

> Then God said, "Let us make man in our image, after our likeness;
> and let them have dominion over the fish of the sea, and over the
> birds of the air, and over the cattle, and over all the earth, and over
> every creeping thing that creeps upon the earth." So God created
> man in his own image, in the image of God he created him; male and
> female he created them.
>
> (vv. 26–27)

In our day these two sentences from the Priestly story of creation
are frequently used as proof texts in the reassessment of what it
means to be human. For some contemporary writers this biblical
passage epitomizes a false view of the place of human beings in the
natural world—a view, it is charged, which is ultimately guilty of
the rape of our planet. The idea of our dominion over all the
earth, ecologists say, does not correspond with reality as we now
know it. The command to fill the earth and subdue it has led to
an unhealthy preoccupation with the uniqueness of humankind.

One regional planner puts his indictment of the Genesis 1 creation story in these words: "Indeed, if one seeks license for those

4

who would increase radioactivity, create canals and harbors with atomic bombs, employ poisons without constraint, or give consent to the bulldozer mentality, there could be no better injunction than this text."[1]

For others who are trying to come to a fresh understanding of human personhood, however, this text has tremendous positive significance. Over against all of the patriarchal baggage of biblical faith, in contrast to the male-oriented bias of most biblical writers, stands this word of cohumanity—"male and female he created them." Read with this emphasis, the creation narrative of Genesis 1 offers strong support for the struggle toward human liberation. Men and women alike rejoice in the equalitarian insight of the Priestly writer. To be created in God's own image, the Bible clearly says, means to be created in and for human partnership.

Neither of these interpretations of Gen. 1:26–27 admits that these two sentences are not fully clear. Therefore, we will begin to think about the question "Who are we?" by looking more closely at this famous and infamous text, and at the idea of the image of God in the Bible as a whole. But we will be looking into a cloudy mirror.

Exegetes, ancient and modern, dealing with the idea of the *imago dei* in the Priestly document recognize at least four persistent questions about what it meant and means. First, what is the significance of the two terms "image" and "likeness"? Second, how is one to understand the plural "Let *us* make man"? Third, where did this idea of the image come from? And, finally and most important, what is the human similarity to God that is here affirmed?

Some early Christian theologians latched onto the presence of the two different terms—image and likeness—with relief. They thought that by distinguishing sharply between them they could understand what had happened to human nature after the Fall of Adam and Eve. The image, they argued, was not lost in the Fall, but the likeness was. According to this perspective, the image was essentially our capacity for rational thought, whereas the likeness was righteousness.

Theologians continued to make such a distinction up through the Reformation and well into the modern period. In the broad sense, they said, we are still fully human after the Fall; but, in the narrower sense, we have lost that likeness to God which the creation story describes. Closely allied with this stress on the difference between the terms, therefore, is the traditional way of discussing biblical anthropology under the rubrics of human being as it was created, as it was corrupted, and as it was or will be restored in Christ. Today it is generally acknowledged that this was an invalid procedure, not only because the text of Genesis does not support it, but also because we human beings can know nothing of human nature in some imagined pre-Fall state. The consensus is that "image" and "likeness" mean essentially the same thing in the Priestly writings. We are not permitted to split that particular theological hair.

The case of the divine plural, "Let *us* make man . . ." is similar. From at least the second century on, Christian writers found clear support for the developed doctrine of the Trinity in this text. Irenaeus comments, "With him always is the Word and Wisdom, the Son and the Spirit, through whom and in whom he freely and spontaneously made all things, and to whom he said, 'Let us make man in our image and likeness.'"[2] Tertullian is equally certain of the meaning of the text when he asks, "How is it possible for someone who is absolutely one and singular to speak in the plural?" He answers, "It was because there was already united to Him as a second Person, his own Word, and a third, the Spirit in the Word, and so he spoke in a plural fashion."[3]

However Trinitarian their theology, modern exegetes are unable to explain the divine plural in this way. Some argue that it is simply an uncensored vestige of the Babylonian creation myth which has influenced Genesis 1. Others, such as Gerhard von Rad, here see the Israelite idea of a heavenly court which is also apparent behind other Old Testament texts.[4]

Whatever traces there may be of a Mesopotamian background, the text as we have it has been decisively altered by Israel's faith in and experience of Yahweh. Israel did not believe that human beings have divine blood in their veins.

Of more interest, therefore, is the question of distinctively Israelite influences to which this idea of human personhood is related. One such possible influence is that of Ezekiel, the prophetic book which stands in closest relationship to the Priestly document.

The prophet speaks cautiously. The one he sees in his vision, seated above the likeness of the throne, is described as "a likeness as it were of a human form" (Ezek. 1:26). James Barr[5] thinks that the writer of Genesis was also influenced by the poet Second Isaiah, especially by his strong contrast between God, the Creator of nature and history, and the idols and images of other nations: "To whom then will you liken God, or what likeness compare with him?" (Isa. 40:18). Or again, "To whom then will you compare me, that I should be like him? says the Holy One" (Isa. 40:25).

In Ezekiel's poetic language, we have the suggestion of an anthropomorphic God which complements the Genesis suggestion of a theomorphous man. In the poetic language of Second Isaiah, there is an emphatic recognition that God is incomparable; he cannot be likened to any image. Yet the poet also speaks in the most blatantly anthropomorphic language. Along with the clear and constant insistence of the Bible that God is not man, Israel's prophetic writers affirmed a fundamental kinship between human beings and the Holy One who had created them.

When the first chapter of Genesis was written, it was not written in a vacuum. Alongside the undoubted influences of other ancient Near Eastern creation epics must be set the experience of Israel itself in its relation to Yahweh. One writer put it in summary form: "Yahweh is so essentially God for and with Israel that *the human is lodged in him.*"[6]

The fourth of the interrelated questions which the notion of an inherent resemblance between humanity and God raises is the thorniest. What *is* the likeness? For centuries traditional theology found it not in the body but in the soul or mind or spirit. It assigned the image language to the spiritual rather than to the physical person. We will have occasion later to return to this unfortunate dualism and its crippling effects on Christian understanding of human selfhood. At this point, however, we need only note that such a distinction is contrary to the Hebraic understanding of human being. Indeed, we cannot rule out the possibility that the Priestly writer intended to include in the image idea what von Rad calls "the marvel of man's bodily appearance."[7] John Calvin shared that opinion. He believed that "there is no part of man, not even his body, which is not adorned with some rays of [God's] glory."[8]

7

Having limited the image to the inner or higher man, in one way or another, most of the early Christian Fathers then went on to try to specify what the resemblance was. For Cyril of Alexandria, writing in the fifth century, for example, the divine image in human beings had six facets: reason, freedom, dominion, sanctification, incorruptibility, and sonship. Given the last of these dimensions, one wonders how Cyril found men and women to be created in the image of God.

Each of these six facets has a long and honorable history in Christian theology. Even today the first three—reason, freedom, and dominion—play a leading role in many interpretations of Gen. 1:26–27. The last three are more likely to be assigned to New Testament texts. But, long before the distinguished Alexandrian theologian was writing about the meaning of the *eikōn* (image), another bishop had rejected this whole cataloging enterprise in strong language. Efforts to localize the divine image, in dominion or elsewhere, said Epiphanius, Bishop of Salamis (A.D. 394), are "drunken belches."[9] Though less graphic in their prose style, theologians today are equally opposed to localizing the image in the "ontic qualities" of human being.

There are two very good reasons for rejecting the older idea of the meaning of the divine image. The first is simply that it presupposes a static view of human nature—a presupposition that today's theologians, influenced in one way or another both by the life sciences and by process philosophy, can no longer accept. A human being is seen today more as an event than as a something. What this implies will become clearer as we proceed.

The other reason is more directly related to biblical interpretation. Why can one not specify the nature of the resemblance between God and human persons indicated by Genesis 1? Because the text does not say what it is. Most exegesis of Gen. 1:26–27 has been what James Barr called a "blood-out-of-stone process."

Acknowledging the reticence about the image in the text itself, some commentators are content to say that it remains a riddle. "The real and true manhood of man is a mystery which comes from God," as one writer expressed it.[10] The point of the image and likeness language is to affirm, not to define, human likeness to God. On the basis of this meager text we cannot tick off a list

[handwritten margin note:] We are at once influenced by time and are time itself

[handwritten note at bottom:] Seemingly contradictory qualities are unified and exist integrally for God; God creates wholeness

8

of human attributes which qualify us for a place in the heavenly council.

What the text does say, unequivocally, is that human beings are creatures. On the sixth day of creation, when the universe is ordered and prepared for the entry of the human species, the verbs of divine creativity change and intensify. The creative fiat of the previous days, "Let there be . . ." gives way to the triple assertion in one verse—God *created* man, he *created* him, he *created* them. God participates "more intimately," as von Rad observes, in this than in the earlier works of creation.

Furthermore, the human creature, according to Genesis 1, is never alone. In contrast to the older story of Genesis 2, where Yahweh creates a living being and subsequently, as it were, decides, "It is not good that man should be alone," this Priestly work understands human being completely as being-in-relationship. There is never an "I" without a "Thou."

No twentieth-century theologians, to my knowledge, have stressed this *relational* aspect of the biblical creation saga more strongly or more incisively than Dietrich Bonhoeffer and Karl Barth. In his compressed meditations on the first three chapters of Genesis, *Creation and Fall*, Bonhoeffer says, "The likeness, the analogy of man to God, is not *analogia entis* but *analogia relationis*. . . . The relation of creature with creature is a God-given relation because it exists in freedom and freedom orginates from God."[11]

Barth marvels, in the third volume of his *Church Dogmatics*, that so many interpreters of "the image of God" could have missed this point, and proceeded to "pure invention in accordance with the requirements of contemporary anthropology."[12] As God's image and likeness we exist as male and female. The sex relationship is the "true *humanum* and therefore the true creaturely image of God." Everything else that can be said about human being "has reference to this plural."

For Barth, the clear statement in the text of what the image of God means, namely, "male and female he created them," is a "great paradigm." From it he develops the notion of human being as *analogia relationis;* human life analogous to the divine form of life. Even as in the triune God there is a harmonious self-encounter and self-discovery, free coexistence and cooperation, open confrontation and reciprocity, so also with humankind. We are "the repetition of this divine form of life; its copy and reflection." The analogy between God and human persons is "simply the existence of the I and the Thou in confrontation." As bearers of the divine form of life, by the grace of God, we are created to live "in open differentiation and joyful relationship."

The phrase, "the image of God," commands a place in the history of Christian theology completely out of proportion to the minor role it plays in the Old Testament. In fact, it is found only in Genesis. In Israel's Wisdom literature of the intertestamental period, however, the idea that human beings are created with a resemblance to the divine being reoccurs. Two passages in the Apocrypha explicitly mention it, and they are in curious contradiction to each other.

In the Wisdom of Jesus ben Sirach (or Ecclesiasticus) the image language is used in a passage which stresses human mortality. In the Wisdom of Solomon it is used to indicate human immortality.

The former passage reads:

> The Lord created man out of earth,
>   and turned him back to it again.
> He gave to men few days, a limited time,
>   but granted them authority over
>   the things upon the earth.
> He endowed them with strength like his own,
>   and made them in his own image.

mortality (Gen. 2)

(Ecclus. 17:1–3)

The chapter continues to reflect on the unique qualities of human beings in their relationships to the Lord, to each other, to nature, and to Israel's history. Some manuscripts add a verse that says that, in addition to giving human beings the five senses, the Lord also gave them the gift of mind and of reason, "the interpreter of his operations." On this reading, the image is closely related to human rationality, as so many early Christian theologians were convinced, and to human "dominion" over the animal kingdom.

The second passage, written by a Hellenistic Jew, probably in Alexandria, tells us that "God created man for incorruption, and made him in the image of his own eternity" (Wisd. of Sol. 2:23). The author goes on to say that death came into the world through

10

"the devil's envy," and that those who belong to the devil's party will die. This same author uses image language in another context, not of the human being but of the divine Wisdom which is a "pure emanation of the Almighty":

Immortality of Wisdom

> For she is a reflection of eternal light
> a spotless mirror of the working of God,
> and an image of his goodness.
>
> (Wisd. of Sol. 7:26)

Here we encounter an idea which comes close to the New Testament reflection on the meaning of the image of God, since the dominant New Testament use of the idea is with direct reference to the person of Jesus Christ.

The New Testament contains two exceptions to this christological understanding of who is the image of God. The first is in the letter of James, in the midst of a discussion about the problems of the human tongue (James 3:9). The second is in Paul's first letter to the Corinthians (11:7), where, in clear contradiction to Genesis 1, we read that woman is *not* made in the image of God. We will return to this extraordinary bit of Pauline thought in the next chapter. For the moment it is worth noting with amusement both the embarrassment the verse caused one interpreter thirty years ago, and the difficulty he had coping with it in intelligible English. The two matters, as we shall see, are closely interconnected:

> . . . we nevertheless hear him say that man as male or husband is God's image and glory, but that man as female or wife is only the glory of the husband. . . . As Paul expresses this idea only once, and that in a desperate effort to preserve the husband's domination over his wife, one may well doubt that he meant it to be given a full theological implication.[13]

In the rest of Paul's writings, however, as well as in Hebrews, the person who in the first instance bears the image, likeness, character, or glory of God is neither the average male nor the average female. Rather it is Jesus Christ, the risen Lord of the Christian community. It is he who shows us what it really means to be human. It is he who tells us what it really means to be created in the image of God. Those who are related to Christ, who are "in Christ," come to share that image.

11

C. K. Barrett duly warns us that it is "impossible to draw together into a unity the various occurrences in the Pauline writings of the word *image*."[14] Nevertheless, we can properly distinguish between Paul's talking about Christ himself as the image of God, and other places in his letters where he talks about the image of believers transformed into the likeness of Christ.

We need to look at both aspects of Paul's thought with some care. In each case he was setting forth a notion of God *in relation* to human beings, fully conscious of the fact that his ideas differed sharply from a very popular alternative view of the place of human beings in the cosmos. It may be anachronistic to label that competing world view in Paul's day "Gnosticism," but he was undoubtedly combating a gnostic type of thought. Such thought is fundamentally pessimistic about the human condition in the givenness of nature and history. In contrast, Paul's view of human beings as they are *related* to God in Christ may justly be called optimistic.

Paul identifies Christ as "the image of God" in two of his letters. In both instances the idea he is trying to convey is that Christ is the one who reveals authentic knowledge of what God is like.

Writing to the troubled church in Corinth, Paul says:

> And even if our gospel is veiled, it is veiled only to those who are perishing. In their case the god of this world has blinded the minds of the unbelievers, to keep them from seeing the light of the gospel of the glory of Christ, who is the likeness of God. For what we preach is not ourselves, but Jesus Christ as Lord, with ourselves as your servants for Jesus' sake. For it is the God who said, "Let light shine out of darkness," who has shone in our hearts to give the light of the knowledge of the glory of God in the face of Christ.
>
> (2 Cor. 4:3–6)

By choosing to render *eikōn* as "likeness" rather than "image" at this point the translators of the Revised Standard Version confirm the conclusion that the two Hebrew terms in Genesis and their Greek equivalents in the Septuagint (LXX) are virtually synonymous. It could equally well read, "Christ, who is the image of God." More important, however, is the double implication of the text. If you look at Christ, you can *see* the glory of God, which is entirely good news. If the Creator who said "let there be light" enlightens your heart, you will *know* the glory of God reflected in the face of Jesus Christ.

12

Whenever I encounter the intimate connection between "seeing" and "knowing," I am reminded of the light bulbs glowing over the heads of Little Orphan Annie and her comic strip friends, denoting what used to be called "the Aha! experience." Paul suggests that experience here. He is talking about revelation, about God making himself known in and through Jesus Christ. He is also being his usual allusive self, as he alludes to the text of Genesis 1 and also to the type of thought about Wisdom which we encountered in the Wisdom of Solomon. As Barrett notes, in late Judaism Wisdom was thought of both as God's agent in creation and as God's agent in conversions. She was the one who entered into holy souls and made them friends of God.

Writing to the Christian church at Colossae, Paul (or one of his followers) uses similarly loaded vocabulary when he says that he has been praying that Christians there may be filled with the knowledge (*gnōsis*) of God's will in all spiritual wisdom and understanding. The opening chapter of Colossians includes what most commentators believe was both a pre-Pauline and a pre-Christian hymn, but one which has been baptized, as it were, by the addition of the doctrine of redemption, the forgiveness of sins.

Whatever its history, the text as we have it makes three assertions about Jesus Christ that deserve our attention:

He is the image of the invisible God, the first-born of all creation (1:15).

In him all things hold together (17b).

He is the beginning, the first-born from the dead (18b).

The first statement claims that Christ is the one who makes known to us what God is like. Revelation rather than cosmological speculation is uppermost. But we also have a statement pregnant with the idea of new creation, a statement parallel to the third assertion with its decided note of promise, of resurrection. The author is talking not just about what happens after human beings die. He is also alluding to a new life, a new creation that is present gift and possibility, as well as something to be fully realized in the future.

The second statement, "In him all things hold together," in its present context is a triumphant denial of gnostic dualism. No splitting of body and soul, of matter and spirit, is possible. All things, "whether on earth or in heaven," have been reconciled through Jesus Christ.

The remaining four uses of *image* in the Pauline corpus which bear on our subject refer more directly to those who profess and call themselves Christians. They form what Barrett calls "a striking set." I will follow his lead in reproducing them together, using his translations (with one emendation).[15]

> Those whom [God] foreknew, he also predestinated to share the image borne by his Son, that he might be the eldest of a large family of brothers [and sisters].
>
> (Rom. 8:29)

> As we have borne the image of the earthly man, we shall bear also the image of the heavenly man.
>
> (1 Cor. 15:49)

> As we all, with unveiled face, behold as in a mirror the glory of the Lord, we are transformed into the same image, from glory to glory.
>
> (2 Cor. 3:18)

> You have put off the old man with his deeds, and put on the new man who is renewed with a view to knowledge in the image of him that created him, where there cannot be Greek and Jew, circumcision and uncircumcision, barbarian, Scythian, bond, free, but Christ is all in all.
>
> (Col. 3:9–11)

Individually, these Pauline texts pose numerous questions for any thoughtful reader. How are we to come to terms with the specter of "we happy few" raised by the Romans quotation? What does he mean by the heavenly man in 1 Corinthians? What, indeed, does glory mean? And are my new possibilities for renewal really just "with a view to knowledge"?

Collectively, however, these texts speak with power about our human present and our human future. They indicate that for Paul, human beings as they are related to Jesus Christ are in the process of radical change and that they should expect change, welcome change, rejoice in change. They indicate further that we have not yet fully discovered what it means to be human, do not yet fully bear (or wear) that image and likeness to God for which we are created and re-created. They summon us to the future. And they

14 * "Christianity is not a conversion experience but a painful revolution" M. McDonald.

make it clear that in <u>Pauline thought</u> as a whole the entire human <u>race is a unity</u>, that we have no grounds for building those fences, of which we are so fond, for keeping other people out.

I have dwelt at length on Paul in the second half of this chapter because his writings are those in the New Testament which have the most to say about the *imago dei* and its expression in and through Jesus Christ. For the author of Hebrews, however, the timeless question of the Psalmist, "What is man that thou are mindful of him?" also finds its answer in Jesus. Jesus is the pioneer of true humanity, the one who delivers the children of God from the power of death and brings them to glory. To that end, he shared our flesh-and-blood nature, our state of being a little lower than the angels. To that end, he became like us "in every respect" (Heb. 2:17). He suffered and he died.

This same Jesus, according to Hebrews, "reflects the glory of God and bears the very stamp of his nature" (1:3). The destiny of faithful women and men is to share God's holiness (12:10). Lest we grow weary in the life of faith, we are exhorted to look to Jesus and what he endured for the sake of the joy that was set before him (12:2).

By now it should be clear why, in my judgment, a Christian anthropology necessarily opens into theology, especially into Christology. I am in agreement on that score with David Jenkins, who, in his Bampton Lectures of 1966 called *The Glory of Man,* reversed the dictum of Ludwig Feuerbach, the nineteenth-century German theologian who was fascinated by the cultural phenomenon of *religion.* Whereas Feuerbach had said that all theology must be understood as anthropology, Jenkins insists that "this is truly so only because all anthropology must be understood as theology."[16]

Our examination of the biblical articulation of the image of God thoroughly confirms this interrelationship. This and other relationships will continue to be at the center of our attention in succeeding pages as we continue to reflect on the question, "Who are we?" made in the image of God.

* now see Galatians 3:28

NOTES

1. Ian L. McHarg, *Design with Nature* (New York: Doubleday & Co., 1969), p. 26.

2. Irenaeus, *Adversus haereses* IV, 20. See John Edward Sullivan, O.P., *The Image of God: The Doctrine of St. Augustine and its Influence* (Dubuque, Iowa: Priory Press, 1963), p. 170.

3. Tertullian, *Adversus Praxean* 12.

4. Gerhard von Rad, *Genesis: A Commentary* (Philadelphia: Westminster Press, 1961), p. 57.

5. James Barr, "The Image of God in the Book of Genesis—A Study in Terminology," *Bulletin of the John Rylands Library* 51 (1968): 11–26.

6. Ulrich Mauser, "Image of God and Incarnation," *Interpretation* 24 (1970): 355. Emphasis added.

7. Mauser, "Image of God," p. 57.

8. John Calvin, *Institutes* I, xv, 3.

9. Walter J. Burghardt, *The Image of God in Man According to Cyril of Alexandria* (Woodstock, Md.: Woodstock College Press, 1957), p. 58.

10. Friedrich Horst, "Face to Face: The Biblical Doctrine of the Image of God," *Interpretation* 4 (1950): 262.

11. Dietrich Bonhoeffer, *Creation and Fall* (London: SCM Press, 1959), p. 37. For another interpretation of Gen. 1:27 in connection with freedom, see Phyllis Trible, *God and the Rhetoric of Sexuality* (Philadelphia: Fortress Press, 1978), pp. 12–23.

12. Karl Barth, *Church Dogmatics* I, 3 (Edinburgh: T. & T. Clark, 1958), p. 193. The following summary is based on pp. 186–193.

13. S. Vernon McCasland, "The Image of God according to Paul," *Journal of Biblical Literature* 69 (1950): 97.

14. C. K. Barrett, *A Commentary on the Second Epistle to the Corinthians* (New York: Harper & Row, 1973), p. 132.

15. C. K. Barrett, *From First Adam to Last: A Study in Pauline Theology* (New York: Charles Scribner's Sons, 1962), p. 97.

16. David Jenkins, *The Glory of Man* (London: SCM Press, 1967), p. 50. For a more recent discussion of Feuerbach in connection with the image of God, see Geoffrey Wainwright, *Doxology: The Praise of God in Worship, Doctrine and Life* (New York: Oxford University Press, 1980), pp. 15–44.

CHAPTER TWO

Male and Female

By locating what is distinctively human in the relationship between male and female, both Karl Barth and Dietrich Bonhoeffer underlined a central and centrally important aspect of the Christian understanding of human being. Human life now and in the future is irreducibly social. Neither the false individualism of much secular thought about the question "Who am I?" nor the false individualism of much so-called Christian thought about the question "What must I do to be saved?" does justice to the biblical understanding of humanity. We are made and we live in the first person plural.

By locating the "image of God" in human sexuality, however, we have raised some very basic questions for theological anthropology—questions which do not yet permit any definitive answers. Furthermore, this interpretation of human creaturehood serves to remind us that human life as we know it is ambiguous. We are invited to live with uncertainty even as we try to seek clarity in understanding ourselves and our world.

Four principal questions arise from this insistence that human being is fundamentally of two kinds: (1) What is the nature of the difference? and (2) What is the nature of the relationship? (3) On what basis can one say that sexuality is distinctively human, since it is so evidently shared with other animals? and (4) How does this

17

definition of the image of God relate to the male human being, Jesus of Nazareth, whom the New Testament says is the perfect image of his heavenly father? These four questions will preoccupy us in this chapter.

Even a few years ago it might have sounded absurd to ask the *first* question, what is the difference between male and female? That seemed self-evident. In the current discussion of human sexuality, the question must be taken seriously. And I think the answer must be that we do not really know.

One aspect of the problem, but only one, is linguistic. When we are talking about the differences between men and women, are we talking about sex or gender? Are we talking, that is, biologically or culturally? An appeal to Webster merely illustrates the problem. The word "sex" in English usage applies both to a biological and to a cultural distinction. It means, in the first instance, either of the two divisions into which persons and animals and plants are divided with reference to their reproductive functions. It also means "all the attributes by which males and females are distinguished."

How then do those attributes distinguish females from males? This current debate is a legitimate one. At one end of the spectrum are the "environmentalists." One reviewer of a feminist diatribe accused the author of thinking that if we ignored our different reproductive organs we would all be the same. Other feminists admit to some additional physiological differences, such as size and strength, but they assert that responsible studies have found no gender-based emotional or intellectual differences.

At the other end of the spectrum are those who believe with Freud that in one way or another anatomy is destiny. Calling upon Sigmund Freud, Erik Erikson, Erich Fromm, and other psychoanalysts for support, Eric Mount, for example, insists that "one's basic biology still involves tendencies and proclivities which are larger than physiological in their ramifications."[1] It is worth noting that he chose to make this statement in an article called "The Feminine Factor," as if a masculine factor were not also in question. For Mount, these "tendencies and proclivities" extend to different ways of *knowing*. Along with split-brain research, exploring the functions of the left and right hemispheres of the brain, some contemporary

18 * And that is cultural and changing.

psychologists are engaged in a controversy over whether male and female brains actually function differently. We will return to this question, as well as to Jungian variations on these themes, in a later chapter.

The behavioral sciences have not yet established, and perhaps in principle never can establish fully, the extent of natural, biological differences between males and females. One physician (arguing against the theory that our future selfhood is determined almost entirely by our anatomy) points to the reason when he lists *eight* variables which help determine human gender identity. Five of them are physical: chromosomal sex, gonadal sex, hormonal sex, accessory internal sex organs, and external genitals. These all play a subordinate role, he claims. The major determinants of gender identity are socio-psychological. These include the sex of assignment and rearing, the core gender identity or psychological self-image, and the gender role identity leading to gender-linked role behavior.[2] By the time children are eighteen months old, they usually have a strong sense of gender identity, and the cultural environment has contributed as much as the biological heritage to their development as girls or boys.

Other evidence from research done by experimental psychologists suggests similar conclusions. One study, for example, found sex role differences in infants from three weeks to three months old related to the amount of mother-child interaction.[3] Since the male infant subjects slept less and cried more than female infants, the mothers spent more time with them in the early weeks. But, since the female infants were easier to comfort, the mothers were positively reinforced for responding to their cries, and came to spend more time with them. Girls were rewarded for dependent behavior; boys, in effect, were forced to become more independent.

Such observations may help explain why play behavior differences can be noted in one-year-old girls and boys—although different toy preferences were not evident in one such study. In the light of such findings, it is easy to see why many people reject Erikson's use of play studies with school-age children as the basis for concluding that females prefer passive "inner space" activities because of their body plan.

* maybe in this study the males slept more.

19

Another finding of psychologists is relevant to our question of the difference between males and females in terms of the cultural influences on their identity. Boys enjoy being boys more than girls enjoy being girls. One study of sex role preferences (although published in 1959) concluded, "The girl quickly learns to prefer the masculine role since our culture . . . is still masculine centered and masculine oriented, and offers the male many privileges and much prestige not accorded the female."[4]

One survey conducted at a large university some years ago asked students whether, if they could have only one child, they would prefer a boy or a girl. Ninety-one percent of the men and sixty percent of the women interviewed said they would want a boy. Things were not much different in the days of the prophet Jeremiah when he cried out,

> Cursed be the man who brought the news to my father, "A son is born to you," making him very glad.
>
> (Jer. 20:15)

But this dimension of sexual inequality cannot all be blamed on biblical patriarchy, as some feminists seem to believe. A Han dynasty poem by Fu Hsuan (A.D. 218–278) from the third century echoes Jeremiah:

> A son is born to be master
> A god from the start . . .
> A girl's birth delights no one
> She's not prized, even at home.

To talk of the cohumanity of males and females as created equally in the image of God does not tell us anything definitive about the differences between them. Theologically, it affirms that there is only one legitimate differentiation between human beings, a point Barth stressed. It thus affirms our individuality—my God-given right to be me and your God-given right to be you. It says nothing about all females or all males in all their manifold variety and complexity. It frees us from all cultural stereotyping. I don't have to become either Total Woman or Wonder Woman. You don't have to become either Total Man or Superman. There are no such people. We become human, we become ourselves, only as we relate to one another.

Clifford Green celebrated this implication of Barthian thought beautifully in an article called "Liberation Theology? Karl Barth on Women and Men."[5] Picking up on Barth's own interest in a theology of human freedom, Green demonstrated—I think conclusively—that Barth's view of the *imago dei* offers a liberating insight. Sharply ridiculing sexual stereotypes, Barth says that they are impossible to defend, however interesting they may be. "Obviously we cannot seriously address and bind any man or woman on these lines."[6]

Yet in other sections of his system, Barth betrayed his own insight, as Green acknowledges. This is especially clear in a now infamous passage where he says,

> The disjunction and the conjunction of man and woman, of their sexual independence and sexual interrelationship, is controlled by a definite order. . . . They stand in a sequence. It is in this that man has his allotted place and woman hers. It is in this that they are orientated on each other. It is in this that they are individually and together the human creature as created by God.[7]

With great care he then stresses once again their equality and the fact that "they become and are free or unfree together."

Nevertheless, Barth continues, there is an order in the relationship. "Order means succession. It means preceding and following. It means super- and sub- ordination."[8] He thinks that this state of affairs does no one any injustice. Yet he says flatly, "in respect of order he is man, and therefore A, and thus precedes and is superior to woman."[9] Woman, of course, is B.

Labeling Barth a blatant misogynist, many readers simply close the book at this point. More perceptive, it seems to me, are the critics who find the source of the problem in Barth's theological method and especially in his treatment of Scripture, rather than in his own cultural upbringing. Green puts his finger on the main issue—that Barth tried to systematize conflicting New Testament texts on the subject of male-female relationships, texts that cannot be harmonized. He refused to recognize, as Green puts it, "the social and historical conditioning which the subordinationist texts presuppose and promote."[10]

One of the most troublesome of those New Testament texts is the image of God passage in 1 Corinthians, the one which we

* A failure of Barth's historical-critical method; a failure to see the setting

21

deferred discussing in the last chapter. It is the passage in which
Paul says: *male (master)*

> But I want you to understand that the head of every man is Christ,
> the head of a woman is her ~~husband~~, and the head of Christ is God.
> . . . For a man ought not to cover his head, since he is the image and
> glory of God; but woman is the glory of man. (For man was not made
> from woman, but woman from man. Neither was man created for
> woman, but woman for man.) (11:3, 7–9)

In context, you remember, Paul seemed to be telling our mothers
that they could not go to church without wearing a hat. What was
he really saying?

The Revised Standard Version has unnecessarily introduced the
notion of the marriage relationship by translating man (male) as
husband in verse 3. According to Hans Conzelmann, among others, it is not a question of marriage being discussed here, but of
the nature of men and women as such. The author is drawing on
a tradition of Hellenistic Jewish speculation that had developed
various series of image/reflection patterns inherited from Plato.
This thought-complex already furnished him with the head, image, and glory (or reflection) chain. In verse 3, a "chain of origi-
nating and subordinating relationships" is set up—God, Christ,
man, woman.[11] And the language connotes a difference of essence.

What matters to the author in this passage, despite a somewhat
confused and confusing argument, is the subordination of woman
to man. Commentators disagree as to the intent of the image-glory
contrast in verse 7, but the allusion in verse 8 to the Adam's rib
story is clear. Thus woman is derivative human being. She is not
the image of God except in a secondary sense. She is created to
serve the male.

Various efforts can be made to circumvent this reading of the
text, or to excuse Paul of responsibility for this idea. Conzelmann
disagrees with Barth's claim that Paul did not want to assert a
difference in the relationships which a woman and a man have
with God. Paul did, indeed. But Conzelmann believes that Paul
could not have derived this idea from Genesis, only from the speculative school of thought which gave him his presuppositions.[12]
Alternatively, one can argue that the text is not written by Paul,
but is a later interpolation into the letter.[13] The very confusion of
the argument helps support this thesis.

Whether Paul was a chauvinist or not, the real issue here is the way in which this and similar subordinationist texts in the canon of Holy Scripture have—through the centuries—shaped the ways in which both women and men think of themselves and of each other.

The misogyny of "the Fathers" is now notorious. Only two examples need be cited by way of reminder. Cyril of Alexandria used this Corinthian passage not to deny that women are in the image of God as well as men, but to assert that since she has it by means of the man, "She differs a little in nature." Adam was more perfect than the woman who was fashioned for his sake.[14] Woman, for Cyril, is "a twittering, loquacious creature with a gift for contriving deceit."[15] St. John Chrysostom thought that man has preeminence both because of his prior creation and because of woman's sin. Only man has the image of God. He is "the king" and should rule over his wife, children, and slaves. Women's service in the home is beneficial because it allows men to participate in public life.[16]

Just ancient thought? Not at all. It is alive and well today in the minds of many church people, as well as among professional theologians. Wolfhart Pannenberg, an eminent member of the latter ranks, sounds almost like St. John Chrysostom when he writes about the division of responsibility between the sexes. Women are connected to the home and men represent the family in relation to the whole of society. Although Pannenberg admits that this is not an immutable arrangement, he believes that "the configuration of the relationship between the sexes in marriage that is traditional for us is extensively appropriate." That includes (from an essay on theological anthropology originally published in 1962) the male's "particular concern" for "the interconnection of the family with the rest of society."[17] Man in outer space and woman in inner space seems to be a correlate of the Pauline and Barthian idea of man first, woman second.

Barth, you recall, labeled man "A." A recent book called *Type A Behavior and Your Heart* describes the dangerous Type A behavior in terms of aggressiveness, impatience, competitiveness, acquisitiveness, and the other trappings of success.[18] These two physicians who criticize Type A behavior, it should be stressed, are both male. Large numbers of the church people who cite Paul and other New Testament subordinationist texts in support of their desire to maintain the status quo are female. Not long ago an issue of *Saturday Review,* discussing the clamor over the Equal Rights Amendment to the Constitution, carried a fitting banner headline on the cover: WOMEN AGAINST WOMEN. The lobbyists against the ratification of the ERA are overwhelmingly church women. They hand their representatives pamphlets with such titles as "God's Simple Plan of Salvation." They are convinced that the divine plan for human beings was and is quite specific: women's place is in the home.

So far in this chapter we have been talking about the difference between males and females and about the relationship between them, especially as the latter has been understood in traditional Christian thought. It is time to address our *third* question, that of our relation to other animals. On what basis can we say that we are distinctively human because God created us in the image of God, male and female? The answer to that question is already implicit in what we have been saying about our difference and about our relationship. Indeed, it is time to talk about culture and about sin.

Human beings are the only animals who develop the kind of intricate structures of symbol systems or patterns of communication which we call cultures. To say that anthropologists, devoted to the scientific study of humankind, are interested in those patterns is virtually a tautology. There are other "social animals" and the extent of our similarity to such creatures—to ants, bees, dolphins—will concern us in a later chapter. But at present we must affirm that one aspect of our similarity to other animals, by virtue of our being fellow creatures, is our finitude. However much we are in the image of God, we are unlike God in that we, along with ants, bees, and dolphins, are born and live and die at a particular time and place. But unlike those fellow creatures, our lives are not predominantly determined by our biological equipment. Rather they are significantly determined by our cultural environment.

We resist this aspect of our finitude. We do not like to admit the degree to which we think what we think, or do what we do, because we live in America in the last quarter of the twentieth century, or that Paul thought what he thought and said what he said because he lived in the Mediterranean world of the first century. We still prefer to think of an unchanging "human nature" relatively un-

24

affected by such incidental matters as place and date of birth. Although part of this resistance is profoundly appropriate to our common humanity, much of it is a refusal of creaturehood, of finitude.

The metaphor of human being as "amphibian" has more than a little merit, but it ceases to be helpful if it suggests that we can crawl out on the dry land of eternity as if we are entirely air-breathing adults. We can and do transcend our rootedness in time and space. We do not escape it. It is not irrelevant to Christian theology that Jesus was born in Judea in the reign of Caesar Augustus. Nor is it irrelevant to Christian theology that 1 Corinthians 11 shows the influence of historically and culturally conditioned thought patterns. Any doctrine of scriptural inspiration which does not take account of this dimension of human finitude cannot be a trustworthy basis for a doctrine of human nature.

Human finitude is not sin. Human refusal to accept our finitude is. The ancient biblical account of the Fall is clear on this score. We continually want to be "as gods." One dominant strand in Christian interpretation of the nature of sin has stressed this over-vaunting aspiration of human beings. What is the root sin? It is pride. More recently, however, theologians have recognized an equal and opposite danger or tendency in human beings. It is not only that we are unhappy to count ourselves a little lower than the angels. Rather, many of us seem unhappy to count ourselves any higher than dolphins, reluctant to claim that we are essentially different from them.

It is noteworthy that in our culture over-vaunting aspiration has long seemed to be chiefly a male temptation. The opposite tendency, that toward insufficient self-affirmation and self-assertion, has appeared to be more generally associated with the female. Can it be that sin and sexuality are linked after all?

Dorothy L. Sayers effectively demolished the traditional answer to this question years ago in her pungent essay, "The Other Six Deadly Sins." (She incidentally points up the danger of generic language when she notes that for the majority of people the generic word "immorality" means one thing and one thing only—lust.) A person, she writes, may be

greedy and selfish; spiteful, cruel, jealous, and unjust; violent and

*It is a part of sin in that we resist being who we are and instead envy God, pretending we are such.

25

> brutal; grasping, unscrupulous, and a liar; stubborn and arrogant; stupid, morose, and dead to every noble instinct—and still we are ready to say of him that he is not an immoral man.[19]

Her report of the young man who asked her to tell him what the other six sins were is reminiscent of Karl Menninger's autobiographical account of the time when The Great Sin was masturbation.[20]

The philosopher Paul Ricoeur has opened up for us a new understanding of the deep-rooted link between sin and sexuality with his profound exploration of the symbolism of evil. He helps us to reread ancient materials with greater insight, such as those in Leviticus 15 about who is clean and who is unclean.

Before seeking to penetrate "the forest of meanings" created by the myth of Adam and Eve, Ricoeur develops a typology for considering the human experience of fault. First comes the notion of defilement and the symbolism of stain; second is the notion of sin; third, that of guilt. He writes eloquently of the ambiguity which is experienced in the "half physical, half ethical fear" that clings to the representation of the impure. The gravity attached to violation of sexual prohibitions lies on this level of defilement, immersed in archaic belief: "An indissoluble complicity between sexuality and defilement seems to have been formed from time immemorial."[21] This complicity lies in the background of all our anthropology and ethics, and it is "the archaism that is most resistant to criticism."

For this reason, Ricoeur thinks that growth in ethical understanding—"a refinement of the consciousness of fault"—cannot come from the sexual sphere of existence, but only from the nonsexual. The human relations created in such spheres as work and politics provide the basis for developing an ethic of justice and love. From this ethic, he argues, we are capable of "turning back toward sexuality, of reevaluating and transvaluing it."[22] But, even so, he warns, the terrors accompanying the primordial associations of sexuality and defilement "continue to prowl" in the consciousness of modern people.

Sin is a different "second moment" in the human experience of fault. That which qualifies the whole notion of sin is the phrase "before God." Sin is a religious, not just an ethical category. What Ricoeur calls the whole rich palette of the knowledge of sin is

26

"vaster than the imperative." The experience is rooted in the encounter of human beings with God, in dialogue with him. It lies
in the reciprocity of "an utterance of God and an utterance of
man."[23]

This understanding of the relational character of sin informs
Ricoeur's discussion of the symbolism of the Adamic myth. He sees
a discrepancy at the heart of the story. It presents two interpretations of civilization and of sexuality. "Every dimension of man—
language, work, institutions, sexuality—is stamped with the twofold mark of being destined for the good and inclined toward evil."
In an incisive sentence, he summarizes his interpretation: "The
ambiguity in man, created good and become evil, pervades all the
registers of human life."[24]

The narrative as we have it in Genesis 3 spreads out this human
experience, the experience of everyone, among three characters—
Eve, the serpent, and Adam. But in the symbolism of the myth,
Eve represents the point of weakness, of human frailty, "of the
least resistance of finite freedom to the appeal of the Pseudo . . ."
which is in each of us. Women who are deeply disturbed by their
demonization in Scripture and in Christian thought to the present
have trouble forgiving the Yahwist for this symbolism. They may,
perhaps, take some small comfort from Ricoeur's conclusion:

> Eve, then, does not stand for woman in the sense of 'second sex.'
> Every woman and every man are Adam; every man and every woman
> are Eve; every woman sins 'in Adam,' every man is seduced 'in' Eve.[25]

This whole biblical myth of the Fall, as Ricoeur and many others
interpret it, concerns both our relationship with God and our common human failure to accept and live in our personhood as creatures given awesome freedom and awesome responsibility. Both
our personal freedom and our personal responsibility "before
God" distinguish us from other animals. These are the facts and
facets of human self-understanding which make it impossible to
reduce the religious experience of sin either to symptoms of mental
illness or to legal violations.

The term "sin" may sound archaic to those who associate it only
with moralistic "Thou shalt nots," including "Thou shalt not enjoy
your sexuality." But in biblical perspective, human creatures confronted by their Creator, summoned by him to stand on their feet

and question him, to respond to his initiative, know themselves to be sinners. We have as yet no evidence that other animals are conscious either of their Creator or of their misuse of his gift of freedom. A dolphin is not a sinner.

But neither is Jesus Christ, according to classical Christian theology. He is said to have been made like us in every way except that as the image of God par excellence he shows us what it means to be fully human, what it means to realize fully our human potential. According to classical Christian theology, Jesus is also the one through whom our sins are forgiven, and the one through whom we are delivered from the seductive, enslaving power of evil.

Both assertions about Jesus the Christ are basic to an understanding of human personhood, creatures who are male and female. The first suggests that we think more about the humanity of Jesus; the second that we think more about his offer of new life today. Together they demand that we look toward our future.

We must bracket the problems which the definitions of the Council of Chalcedon (A..D. 451) pose for our modern or postmodern minds in thinking about Jesus Christ. We do not here need to try to unravel the paradox of two natures in one person there affirmed. But we must reemphasize the claim of Christian faith that Jesus was completely human. He was not a divine figure masquerading as a Palestinian Jew. He was not a hermaphrodite in the sense of being a combination of diverse elements, confused and comingled. He was, in every respect, one in being with us. Yet he did not succumb as we do to the temptation to distort reality.

What he was as a human being we too can be—with his help. What he did as a human being, we too can do—with his help. It is necessary to belabor this point because so much of Christian theology has taught us to think of Jesus as not really and truly a human being. Indeed, one fully respectable school of thought still holds that he was not *a* human being in our sense of the word at all, but rather *Homo* in some impersonal, generalized sense. I submit that if this were the case, Jesus would not and could not show us what it means to be human, what it means to be in the image of God.

If, on the other hand, he was actually an individual human person, with a fully human personality, as I believe he was, then he had to be both a culturally conditioned person and a sexual one. He may indeed be our contemporary. He may indeed reappear on the streets of Chicago or New Orleans or Spokane every day and go unrecognized. He may indeed reappear at his second coming in some other form, perhaps as a woman, as Robert Brightman suggested.[26] But when he walked the streets of Capernaum, he was not wearing a halo. He probably needed a bath. He certainly knew about *erōs*.

It is almost necessary to put things that crudely to counteract centuries of Docetism—of thinking that Jesus was not entirely flesh of our flesh and bone of our bone, but only *seemed* so. The man who was executed on a cross outside Jerusalem in the second decade of the common era was fully human. Between his birth and his death, he, like us, had to grow up.

Along with such stress on the radical particularity of Jesus' humanity, therefore, must go an equal stress on the fact that he was a male. Christian theology has been very reticent about Jesus' sex life. The gospels are almost entirely silent on the subject. When Tom Driver of Union Theological Seminary chose to discuss it some years ago, his article won a place in the series called *New Theology*.[27]

Novelists who take seriously this aspect of Jesus' human life are often met by shocked surprise. When Nikos Kazantzakis's *The Last Temptation of Christ* was translated more than a decade ago, a novel in which Jesus is pictured as going through all the sexual turmoil of adolescence, college students read and discussed it with avid interest because it was to them a totally new thought—as well as one which seemed slightly blasphemous.

What Jesus's relationship was with Mary Magdalene or any of the other women mentioned in the gospels we do not fully know. We do not necessarily have to think of him as a feminist, either, although a strong case can be built for that designation. As Hans Küng comments, he showed not only a lack of contempt for women, but a remarkable openness toward them.[28] He appears in the gospel records as one who accepted women's need to experience the everydayness of mere human personality. Jesus treated people as people.

29

Jesus is not merely an example of how to become fully human, however. As Christian faith understands him, he empowers us to open ourselves to others in the same manner. Earlier in this chapter we took a hard look at one of the subordinationist texts in the New Testament, arguing that it must be understood in its sociocultural context. It must also be understood in its theological context.

The subordination theme was clearest in 1 Cor. 11:9 "neither was man created for woman, but woman for man." That statement is counterbalanced almost immediately: "Nevertheless, in the Lord woman is not independent of man nor man of woman" (v. 11). "In the Lord," in relation to the risen Christ, we are freed from having to put one another up on pedestals or down on the kitchen floor. This Corinthian text belongs alongside the now over-familiar text of Gal. 3:27–28. There Paul sounds as if our maleness and femaleness were abrogated in Christ. Here, however, a new mutuality is affirmed.

Made in the image of God, we are social beings. Made in the image of God we are sexual beings, mysteriously different from each other, and yet less than fully personal, fully human, until we learn to relate to one another as equals. In our escape from freedom, we pervert our sexuality, fearfully hiding behind the fig leaves of domination and submission. In our new freedom in Christ we are able to claim afresh our cohumanity. We may even learn to listen to his Word and to speak the truth to one another in love.

NOTES

1. Eric Mount, "The Feminine Factor," *Soundings* 53 (1970): 380.

2. E. Mansell Pattison, "Notes on the Current Quest for Gender Identity," *Journal of Religion and Health* 14 (1975): 82–95.

3. Howard A. Moss, "Sex, Age, and State as Determinants of Mother-Infant Interaction," in Judith Bardwick, *Readings on the Psychology of Women* (New York: Harper & Row, 1972) pp. 22–29.

4. David A. Lynn, "A Note on Sex Differences in the Development of Masculine and Feminine Identification," *Psychological Review* 66 (1959): 129.

5. Clifford Green, "Liberation Theology? Karl Barth on Women and Men," *Union Seminary Quarterly Review* 29 (1974): 221–231.

30 * Being Christian does not mean we return to obeying "the law", invent a new law or become holy by adopting a certain role lock, stock + barrel. Rather it mean

6. Karl Barth, *Church Dogmatics* IV, 3 (Edinburgh: T. & T. Clark, 1960), p. 153.

7. Ibid., pp. 168–169. Green, in "Liberation Theology?" p. 229, calls attention to possible faulty translation in this passage but it does not really alter the meaning.

8. Ibid., p. 169.

9. Ibid., p. 170.

10. Green, "Liberation Theology?" p. 230.

11. Hans Conzelmann, *1 Corinthians*, Hermeneia-A Critical and Historical Commentary on the Bible (Philadelphia: Fortress Press, 1975), p. 184. Cf. C. K. Barrett, *A Commentary on the First Epistle to the Corinthians* (New York: Harper & Row, 1968), p. 246.

12. Conzelmann, *1 Corinthians*, p. 188.

13. See William O. Walker, Jr., "1 Corinthians 11:2–16 and Paul's Views of Women," *Journal of Biblical Literature* 94 (1975):94–110.

14. Cyril of Alexandria, *In epis. 1 ad Corin. 4, 4* as cited by Walter J. Burghardt, *The Image of God in Man According to Cyril of Alexandria* (Woodstock, Md.: Woodstock College Press, 1957), p. 134.

15. Cyril of Alexandria, *De adoratione 1*, as cited ibid., p. 129.

16. Elizabeth A. Clark, "Sexual Politics in the Writings of John Chrysostom," *Anglican Theological Review* 59 (1977): 3–20.

17. Wolfhart Pannenberg, *What is Man? Contemporary Anthropology in Theological Perspective* (Philadelphia: Fortress Press, 1970), p. 93.

18. Meyer Friedman and Ray H. Rosenman, *Type A Behavior and Your Heart* (New York: Alfred A. Knopf, 1977).

19. Dorothy L. Sayers, *Christian Letters to a Post-Christian World* (Grand Rapids, Mich.: Wm. B. Eerdmans Publishing Co., 1969), p. 138.

20. Karl Menninger, *Whatever Became of Sin?* (New York: Hawthorn Books, 1975).

21. Paul Ricoeur, *The Symbolism of Evil* (Boston: Beacon Press, 1969), p. 28.

22. Ibid., p. 29.

23. Ibid., p. 51.

24. Ibid., p. 246.

25. Ibid., p. 255.

26. Robert Brightman, "The Other Half of God," *Religion in Life* 43 (1974): 68–78.

27. Tom Driver, "Sexuality and Jesus," reprinted in M. E. Marty and D. G. Peerman, eds., *New Theology No. 3* (New York: Macmillan Publishing Co., 1966), pp. 118–132.

28. Hans Küng, "Fundamental Theological Ideas," *New York Times Magazine* (May 23, 1976), p. 35.

and struggle with the remnants of what God created

31

CHAPTER THREE

The Ambiguities
of Language

As human beings we talk with each other. We use a variety of gestures for the purpose, but primarily we use our tongues. We speak. We use verbal language.

If there were any single answer to our questions "Who are we? What does it mean to be human?" the answer would have to be linguistic. Anthropologists agree widely that it is language which makes human animals different from other mammals. Claude Lévi-Strauss, the noted French anthropologist, says that whoever says "human" says "language."[1] Language is the hallmark of our human being which is social being.

Psychologists concur. The "most peculiarly human of hominid features," as one expressed it, is speech and language. Speech makes us different from the apes. Philosophers from Plato to Ludwig Wittgenstein have speculated about the mysterious power of language. Theologians from the author of the Fourth Gospel to our contemporary Gerhard Ebeling have meditated on the mystery of word and Word.

And, in spite of this agelong fascination with human speech, we still do not know very much about it. There is still no satisfactory, generally accepted theory as to what language is, much less as to how it evolved in the human species or how it now operates. Anyone beginning to think seriously about the subject encounters

32

what Ebeling aptly calls "the jungle of the problem of language."[2]

In current understanding of this distinctively human phenomenon, two prominent themes are of fundamental importance to any theological reflection on our ability to speak to each other. Both of them have similarities to some of the themes we discussed in the last chapter, similarities which are not likely to be accidental. Both *intercourse* and *discourse,* as George Steiner observes, arise from "the life need of the ego to reach out and comprehend" another human being.[3] The first theme is that language is a biocultural phenomenon. We are rooted in nature. The second theme is that language is both a blessing and a curse. Like sexuality, language is ambiguous. It has no single clear-cut meaning.

The biological basis of our capacity to speak to and listen to another is clear. It depends in part on the architecture of the human mouth and throat and ear, as well as on the specialized development of those parts of the human brain concerned with speech formation and reception. Human infants are born with the capacity to make sounds. When they are still in the babbling and cooing stage, there is no evidence of any cultural difference in the range and sequence of those sounds: "The frequency spectra of the phonemes are practically identical."[4]

All babies, that is, can make vowel sounds, they can make consonant sounds, and they can make variations on both. After a child is five to six months old, however, the spectrum of sounds shifts toward the sound patterns adults use in the child's hearing. Culture, that is, has entered language formation.

It is always tempting to speculate about the possible relationships between the development of any capacity in the growth of the individual and the same capacity in the evolution of the species. But in the case of language development, no one really knows how or why Homo sapiens developed the capacity to formulate and use the symbol systems we call languages. It is agreed that it had something to do with encephalization, with the increase in the size and importance of the brain. The evolutionary enlargement of our brains began, it is said, about three million years ago, and emerged as the *human* brain about 250,000 years ago. It also has something to do with our sensory and motor systems.

One scientist has come up with a theory of why hominids developed the "unusual adaptation" of speech and language which he terms a "supersensory system." His theory, admittedly speculative, is important for what we will be saying later about one of the blessing dimensions of speech. His fundamental thesis is that language did not evolve as a communication device, but to supplement our other sensory systems "for the construction of a real world."[5]

He seems to be saying that when our ancestors came down out of the trees they occupied a niche comparable to that of baboons or wolves. What wolves evolved in order to live successfully as advanced carnivores was a superb sense of smell. What the primates developed was a keen sense of sight. What Homo sapiens developed, in addition, was a capacity for imagery.

Whereas wolves marked their territory with urine, Homo sapiens marked theirs visually and vocally. They learned to map and to name. "By appropriate vocalization one animal in a group could evoke images of geographical maps. . . . It is in such shared imagery, rather than communication in the usual sense, that I would identify the beginning of speech and language."[6] Human languages evolved, we are being told, because human beings had to become storytellers in order to survive.

Whatever plausibility this theory may have, it clearly shows the dangers of a reductive simplification in any theory of language. The dawn of speech remains shrouded in fog. The gap between the wolf's olfactory abilities and the "Song of Deborah" is too great to bridge with a formula. It may well be, as Steiner argues, that a genuine science of language in the future must be based on neurochemical and neurophysiological study. It may be that "a more penetrating neurochemical and electrophysiology of the brain" will throw further light on human linguistic competence. But it is also true, as he himself concludes, that today we can call the study of language an exact science only by stretching the term out of shape.

Arthur Koestler alerts us to the same danger of reductionism. In his exhaustive study of *The Act of Creation,* he reports on what he calls "the cruder forms of Paleo-Behaviorism."[7] In the twenties, J. B. Watson conditioned a five-months-and-twenty-days-old infant to say "da" whenever it was given a bottle. (That "it" is in the Koestler text; it calls for a red flag as we move toward more theological understanding of human relationships through language.)

34

Lest anyone think that such a notion of the heart of language is outmoded (and for comic relief), Koestler appends an extract from a 1961 college textbook on psychology. The book analyzes a snippet of conversation between a man and a woman. It is clearly a series of S-R (Stimulus and Response) connections. The textbook alleges that such "complex activities" as the conversation between two human beings (or the memorization of a poem) can best be studied by bar-pressing experiments "under the more ideal conditions of the laboratory."

The human sciences have much to teach us about the complexities of our capacity to speak a true word. They rightly call us to recognize its dual character, as rooted in our physiological makeup and in our cultural environment. When we want to go more deeply into the meaning of language for you and for me, however, we have to move beyond the so-called ideal conditions of the laboratory into the fuzzier territory of everyday life.

Everydayness was paramount in the snatch of conversation which Koestler chose to quote from the college textbook:

He: What time is it?
She: Twelve o'clock.
He: Thank you.
She: Don't mention it.
He: How about lunch?
She: Fine.[8]

This is such a bare-bones sample of verbal interchange that I think we can helpfully use it as a springboard for looking at three facets of the dark powers of our speech.

Let us start with her "Don't mention it," with the alienation inherent in human language. That banal idiom epitomizes our capacities for using language to shut the other person out, to brush him off, to reject his offer of outreach, to refuse to hear his meaning. It captures our confusion of tongues.

We are dealing here with a single encounter between a man and a woman, but we are also dealing with the story of humankind which on one basic level is the story of confused speech. Why should his straightforward "Thanks" evoke her twisted response, "Don't mention it"? Why be devious? Why can't we say what we mean and hear what the other means, accepting his thanks? We must once more go back to Genesis, back to the biblical diagnosis of our common condition.

According to the Yahwist's account of our language problems in Gen. 11:1–11, there was a time when the whole world had the same language and the same words. The people said, "Come, let us build ourselves a city. . . . let us make a name for ourselves." The author is using an old literary tradition of the Mesopotamian world to make some theological comments on the human situation. We are apt to lose his point if we focus narrowly on the tower with its top in the heavens. In its present context, this is not primarily a Promethean myth.

As the story continues, Yahweh comes down to see the city. And he says:

> If this is how they have started to act, while they are one people with a single language for all, then nothing that they may presume to do will be out of their reach. Let me, then, go down and confound their speech there, so that they shall not understand one another's talk.

(Gen. 11:6–7 according to E. A. Speiser's
Anchor Bible translation of Genesis)

As is well known, the punch line uses a wordplay on the Hebrew Babel (or Babylon) and *balal* (confuse, confound, or mix). The story ends, "That is why it was named *Babel,* since Yahweh *confounded* the speech of the whole world, as he dispersed them from there over the whole world" (11:9).

Every culture has some myth to account for the multitude of human languages. In general, these myths offer two explanations. Either there was some primal accident which plunged humanity into linguistic chaos, or else the gods are punishing us for some reason—such as for eavesdropping on their conversation. It is standard to read this Genesis account as just another such attempt to account for at least 4000 languages (a conservative estimate) in use in the world today. And most of us are fullly at home in only one.

Intriguing as it is to speculate why people in New Guinea, for example, speak in hundreds of different tongues, that is not the central question the biblical story is trying to answer. Rather, the Yahwist is talking chiefly about our alienation from God and from each other. His first stress is on our wanting to make a name *for*

36

Genesis is not the origin of language but the origin of language problems.

ourselves, on our wanting independence from our Creator. The contrast is evident just a few paragraphs later when Yahweh tells Abraham that *he* will make Abraham's name great (12:2). The second stress is on our resulting inability to understand what the other person says. As Jacques Ellul points out, Genesis does not say that there will be lots of foreign languages in the world. The emphasis is on noncommunication, on the fact that people cannot understand each other even when they speak the same language and use the same words.[9]

One of the reasons we do not understand each other is that we use language as much to conceal the truth, to hide ourselves, as we do to communicate the truth, to reveal ourselves. It is fashionable these days to talk about being open and honest, but often glib injunctions to "let it all hang out" fail to recognize the complex way language functions.

Take, for example, the everyday question, "How are you?" If everyone answered it openly and honestly, the economy would grind to a halt. Conventional answers to conventional questions have their social utility.

Furthermore, there is a deeply private aspect of language, one which makes it incredibly difficult to be sure of mutual understanding. Suppose the other person answers your question as if you really wanted to know and says, "I have a headache today." Can you be sure that you both have the same threshold of pain, the same meaning for the word "headache"?

Even our individual understandings of how a word relates to a concept change as our experience grows. Arthur Koestler illustrates this point nicely by introducing a child who asks what a "seductress" is. The child gets the answer, "A very bad woman who uses too much makeup." The word remains unchanged, but the concept later undergoes drastic alteration. The word "seductress" is fixed, Koestler says, but the passengers are constantly changing, getting into and out of the bus. In fact, we may even distinguish between "trim denotations, furtive connotations, and stowaways hidden under the seats."[10] He finds steel barriers to communication and creative thinking in over-fixation on words.

Far more radical is the theory George Steiner develops, brilliantly and at length, in *After Babel.* He thinks that a basic function of language is to help us hide from one another. "Languages conceal and internalize more, perhaps, than they convey outwardly. Social classes, racial ghettos speak at rather than to each other."[11] Those who remember the television series "Up Stairs/Downstairs" will understand his first point. Arcane language is not limited to racial or social ghettos, however. Every profession, every club, every student group, every church denomination has its own.

Steiner also explores the ways in which languages work to keep ages and sexes separated. Childhood has its secret parlance, its deliberate rejection of adult norms of grammar and vocabulary. Read *Huckleberry Finn*. Ethnolinguists are just beginning to study childhood speech and that of women. In a number of cultures men and women use different vocabularies and different grammars. He wonders why this should be, and why men have always charged women with talking too much. "Before the Fall, man and woman may have spoken the same tongue, comprehending each other's meaning perfectly," he comments, "Immediately after, speech divided them."[12]

Is it possible, then, that speech has a hermetic function—serving to keep "the other" at arm's length, serving to keep the "in group" or "we group" communicating, but the "out group" or the "they group" locked outside? Steiner concludes that this is the solution to the age-old problem of Babel. "Words are the living eyes of secrecy," he says, quoting the Russian, Velimir Khlebnikov. The word began largely as "a password, granting admission to a nucleus of like speakers."[13] The primary thrust of language is inward, not outward.

If language is by nature centripetal to the extent Steiner believes it is, we can understand more deeply what a *Washington Post* columnist called the "He/She Dilemma." Why men, confronted with the pain and alienation women are experiencing with customary usage of our language, simply say: consult Webster—"Man" is generic. Why women say that this "generic" is not an inclusive, but an exclusive term, making them invisible and inaudible, nonbeings. The alienating power of language passes easily over into its destructive power. Nelle Morton used no "mere" metaphor when she wrote, "It is killing women not to be heard."[14]

Remember that laconic exchange between a "she" and a "he" we are thinking about? On first glance, it does not appear to show any language that deserves to be called destructive. But look again. Focus on the two lines.

He: What time is it?
She: Twelve o'clock.

This is steno-language, as flat as the Great Salt Desert. It denies both the fullness of human possibility and the capacity of language to help us break through to that possibility, to go outside of ourselves into the joyful freedom of love. Robot language is subhuman. It ignores the freshness and wonder and surprise of words, the creative power of discovering that a sharply turned phrase can open new windows on reality.

Language was better off, perhaps, in the days when people thought that uttering a curse had power to do more than shock their grandmothers. Biblical thought, as well as occult thought about language through the centuries, warns us of dark linguistic powers. As the Epistle of James notes, we use the same mouth to bless God and curse men who are made in the likeness of God (3:9). The Old Testament is shot through with the antithesis between blessing and cursing. The New Testament, too, knows that saying "Let it be anathema!" has the power to cut one off from relationships. Witches who cast spells and priests who seemed to work hocus-pocus tell us that words are potent. They can be used to manipulate the universe. Drawing a chalk line on the floor and reversing the divine Tetragrammaton invited Death.

Language, that is, has the power to destroy as well as the power of self-transcendence. When that is forgotten, language is wearing out. We are left with the taste of words turning to dust in our mouths like rotten mushrooms.[15] Just as when Alice nibbled the mushroom in Wonderland, we shrink. We are reduced to saying nothing more to each other than, "How about lunch?"

If language can be alienating, destructive, and opaque, it can also be communicative, creative, and numinous. Through speech we can be present with and for one another. Through words we can come to see reality anew. Through the power of the Word we are able to have life and have it more abundantly.

The category of *presence* is a helpful one in thinking about the positive features of the gift of language. Consider just our everyday experience of good conversation with a friend. It knits us together in a way that is self-authenticating. We know the other person is there, with us. Because of having been together and having come to know one another through the self-revelation of speech, we are able to enjoy companionable silence. Conversely, we can almost always tell when the other person is not "there," even though the talk goes on. When the other person has ceased listening and is busily engaged with private thoughts, it is almost as if a physical presence had been withdrawn.

Think also of the sense of personal presence which comes in and through receiving a good letter. Sometimes even just a postcard in a familiar handwriting can do the trick. The double meaning of correspondence is instructive. It rightly means both communication by letter and the agreement of things with one another. As the telephone company never lets us forget, a long distance call also works its magic. The living voice closes spaces between us.

For Gerhard Ebeling "'the presence' of the hidden indicates what the distinctive function and power of language consists of."[16] It can bridge the space between human beings, both literally and figuratively; it can also transcend the present moment. Through language we are able to summon the past into the present. Through language we are also able to anticipate the future. Language draws us into community not only with our current neighbors but also with the whole company of saints and sinners that we call the human race—past, present, and future.

Reflection on our everyday experience of presence can help us understand what a number of contemporary theologians are saying both about what it means to be human and about what Christian tradition means when it calls Jesus Christ the Word of God. Again Christology illuminates anthropology and vice versa.

We can no longer think of the "essence" of a person as something found in interior self-consciousness or cognition. It is found rather in "the reflexive movement between self and world, a movement mediated by language."[17] Through language we are open to the world, to reality. Our basic situation is a word situation. In that situation, the human voice is presence. The sound of the human voice can communicate from my interior to your interior, from

40

your heart to my heart. As Ebeling put it, "language is the body of our spirit."[18]

As we think about language, we recognize, furthermore, that we are not self-sufficient. We are dependent on our brothers and sisters. Even as we received the gift of language taught to us by others, so we in turn long to hear an answer to our own speaking.

Similarly, to call Jesus Christ "Word of God" is not to talk about some supernatural substance. It is to talk about a word event that is the medium of God's presence in the world. If, as Martin Heidegger said, "language is the 'house of being,' so is word the event of being itself." Thus, according to Christian tradition, Word of God "seeks to be understood as a word event that does not go out of date, but constantly renews itself, does not create closed areas of special interest but opens up the world, does not enforce uniformity but is linguistically creative."[19] Or, as the author of Hebrews put it, "In many and various ways God spoke of old to our fathers by the prophets; but in these last days he has spoken to us by a Son, whom he appointed the heir of all things, through whom also he created the world" (1:1–2).

God is the one who has "word" absolutely. Revelation is not a body of truths from another world. It is an event of door-opening in the world. He is the one who communicates himself. As the power rather than the object of disclosure, he also empowers us to disclose ourselves before him and to each other. Whatever else the text may mean, that is one clear consequence of the gospel report about Jesus: "And they were astonished beyond measure, saying, 'He has done all things well; he even makes the deaf hear and the dumb speak'" (Mark 7:37).

As Word of God Jesus is presence and power with us. As Word of God Jesus demonstrates communication. As Jesus of Nazareth he teaches us how to speak creatively. Two aspects of Jesus' own use of language as we know it from the gospels command our attention. First, he used words to include, not to exclude people. Second, he used words to surprise them.

The variety of people Jesus talks with in the gospels is astonishing: rich tax collectors and blind beggars, prostitutes and priests, lawyers and lepers, Roman army officers and psychotics, children and religious leaders, sick women and working women and foreign

* my emphasis on prayer as a theological statement.

41

women and family women. The tradition remembers that he addressed many of these people, not just those in his immediate circle of friends, by name. It remembers also that when he spoke "his word was with authority" (Luke 4:32).

Nothing is better attested to in the gospels than that Jesus was a story teller. Matthew's gospel goes so far as to say that he said nothing to the crowds without a parable (13:34). Parables are extraordinarily hard to live with, however. Even before the New Testament was finished, the church had turned some of Jesus' parables into allegories, or good moral example tales, or audio-visual aids to timeless truths. Preachers have been doing the same things to them ever since.

In recent years many people have been rediscovering that Jesus used parables as linguistic art, as poetic metaphor, to express a new vision of the world and to invite his listeners to participate in that experience. Thus parables cannot be translated into generalizations such as "God loves everyone." Neither can they be demythologized, since they are not mythic.

With help from Marianne Moore, John Dominic Crossan makes that point tellingly. A myth, he says, "gives us imaginary gardens with imaginary toads in them." A parable, in contrast, "gives us imaginary gardens with real toads in them."[20] The juxtaposition of the extraordinary and the ordinary is potent. Through it, as Sallie McFague argues, the transcendent comes to ordinary experience and disrupts it.[21]

Crossan's *In Parables* carries the subtitle, "The Challenge of the Historical Jesus." One level of that challenge is to our boredom with words; a second is to the quality of our experience. Crossan believes that Jesus spoke in metaphoric parables because he experienced God in the joy of language:

> There is an intrinsic and inalienable bond between Jesus' experience and Jesus' parables. A sensitivity to the metaphorical language of religious and poetic experience and an empathy with the profound and mysterious linkage of such experience and such expression may help us to understand what is most important about Jesus: his experience of God.[22]

Biblical scholars have long recognized that the function of Jesus' parables was to proclaim the inbreaking of the kingdom of God, and that parables call upon us to rethink our notions of time. Instead of thinking about time on the model of railroad tracks running straight from the past to the future, the parabolic view of time is comparable to the several staves on a musical score. Crossan discusses Jesus' parables under three rubrics: Parables of Advent, of Renewal, and of Action. All three types are evident, however, in a single verse from Matthew:

> The kingdom of heaven is like treasure hidden in a field, which a man found and covered up; then in his joy he goes and sells all that he has and buys that field.
>
> (13:44)

Crossan's interpretation of this verse deserves quotation at some length:

> We are confronted, for example in the Treasure parable, with a man whose normalcy of past-present-future is rudely, but happily shattered. The future he had presumably planned and projected for himself is totally invalidated by the *advent* of the Treasure which opens up new worlds and unforeseen possibilities. In the force of this advent he willingly *reverses* his entire past, quite rightly and wisely he sells "all that he has." And from this advent and this reversal he obtains the Treasure which now dictates his time and his history in the most literal and concrete sense of these words. It gives him a new world of life and action he did not have before and he could not have programmed for himself.[23]

Through Jesus' creative use of language, the listeners have their own world turned upside down. Jesus announces God as the shatterer of their presuppositions about human social structures. They discover that the kingdom *is* in advent, that "it is surprise and it is gift."[24] He challenges them to act and live from that gift.

Language, we have claimed, is what makes us human. It is that dimension of our creaturehood which most sharply shows our interdependence one with another, and our difference from other animals. Language is charged with mysterious powers. When we misuse it, it can separate us from each other and from the wellspring of our being. Our capacity to misuse it can, in fact, kill it, just as it can be used to wound, to isolate, to cut off other persons.

Recognized as a gift from the other, accepted with thanks, and used with fear and trembling, on the other hand, language can

43

open us to new and surprising communion with all that is beyond us. The life-giving power of language is well confirmed by the person and practice of Jesus. When we think of him as one who shows us the positive powers of language, we move from the prosaic to the poetic. And poetic, as Paul Ricoeur insists, means more than poetry as a literary genre. "Poetic means creative."[25]

Beyond the powers of the word to communicate presence and to reshape our views of reality, however, lies a life-giving quality of the word which is independent of printers' conventions. It does not matter, in my judgment, whether or not one chooses to think a capital letter on Helen Keller's discovery of word. Her account of her experience of W-A-T-E-R vibrates with the tones and overtones thousands of Christians have used to sing of their experience with the one whom they call Word. If we needed any further reminder of the symbolic character of language, Helen Keller provides it. She also gives us, gifts us, with a superb example of what can happen when the ordinary and the extraordinary come together. As her teacher put one of her hands under running water and spelled into the other, Keller remembers:

> Suddenly I felt a misty consciousness of something forgotten—a thrill of returning thought; and somehow the mystery of language was revealed to me. I knew then that "w-a-t-e-r" meant the wonderful cool something that was flowing over my hand. That living word awakened my soul, gave it light, joy, set it free! . . . As we returned to the house each object that I touched seemed to quiver with life. That was because I saw everything with the strange new sight that had come to me.[26]

Insofar as we are human, we are summoned to the limits of language and beyond them.

NOTES

1. Edmund Leach, *Claude Lévi-Strauss* (New York: Penguin Books, 1974), p. 37.

2. Gerhard Ebeling, *Introduction to a Theological Theory of Language* (Philadelphia: Fortress Press, 1973), pp. 81–128.

3. George Steiner, *After Babel: Aspects of Language and Translation* (New York: Oxford University Press, 1975), p. 38.

4. Arthur Koestler, *The Act of Creation* (New York: Dell Publishing Co., 1967), p. 594.

5. Harry J. Jerison, "Evolution of the Brain," in M. C. Wittrock et al., *The Human Brain* (Englewood Cliffs, N.J.: Prentice-Hall, 1977), p. 55.

6. Ibid., p. 57.

7. Koestler, *Creation*, p. 594.

8. Ibid., p. 603. The "conversation" is quoted from A. D. Calvin, ed., *Psychology* (Boston: Allyn and Bacon, 1961), p. 375.

9. Jacques Ellul, *The Meaning of the City* (Grand Rapids, Mich.: Wm. B. Eerdmans Publishing Co., 1970), p. 19.

10. Koestler, *Creation*, p. 600.

11. Steiner, *After Babel*, p. 32.

12. Ibid., p. 43.

13. Ibid., p. 321.

14. Nelle Morton, "The Rising Woman Consciousness in a Male Language Structure," *Andover Newton Quarterly* 13 (1972): 190. This was a seminal article for studies which now fill a five-foot shelf.

15. See Ebeling, *Theory of Language*, p. 69 and Steiner, *After Babel*, pp. 184ff. The simile originated with Hugo von Hofmannsthal, whom both writers cite independently.

16. Ebeling, *Theory of Language*, p. 54.

17. Peter C. Hodgson, *Jesus—Word and Presence* (Philadelphia: Fortress Press, 1971), p. 136.

18. Gerhard Ebeling, *God and Word* (Philadelphia: Fortress Press, 1966), p. 29.

19. Ibid., p. 40.

20. John Dominic Crossan, *In Parables: The Challenge of the Historical Jesus* (New York: Harper & Row, 1973), p. 15.

21. Sallie McFague, *Speaking in Parables: A Study in Metaphor and Theology* (Philadelphia: Fortress Press, 1975), p. 23.

22. Crossan, *In Parables*, p. 22.

23. Ibid., p. 34.

24. Ibid., p. 51.

25. Paul Ricoeur, "Listening to the Parables of Jesus," *Criterion* (1974): 21.

26. Helen Keller, *The Story of My Life*, as quoted by Koestler, *Creation*, p. 222.

CHAPTER FOUR

Working and Playing

Because we are people created in the image of God we also work and play together. We are related to each other as human beings not only through discourse and intercourse, but also through sharing in labor and leisure. In addition to considering shared sexuality and shared language as definitive of our humanity, our essentially social being, we must think about the ways we "spend our time" together.

For centuries men and women have thought of themselves in relation to their work, what they do for a living. They have understood themselves as people who build or make something, as *Homo faber*. A man may call himself a builder by trade, a woman may call herself a homemaker. The difference is slight. The emphasis has been on ourselves as fabricators—builders and makers.

More recently, perceptive critics of our culture have asked us to think of ourselves also as *Homo ludens,* people who share the gift of play. And they have strongly suggested that we need to discover and practice a better balance in our lives between labor and leisure, a more graceful harmony between those two rhythms of our co-humanity. That dimension of our human partnership demands closer attention.

The New Yorker, a modern guide to the perplexed, has published a trio of cartoons in recent years which help focus the issues that contemporary Christians must address. Their captions locate another thicket of theological questions about anthropology.

The *first* is in colonial dress. A woman sits locked in the stocks, knitting. Two Pilgrim-costumed men pass by. One says to the other, "Sinner though she be, it's heartening to see she remains faithful to the work ethic." The *second* pictures a man on the psychiatrist's couch. The caption is, "My Protestant work ethic made me a bundle, but my Puritan guilt complex wouldn't let me enjoy it." The *third* shows a man hanging up his coat in the hall closet, speaking over his shoulder to his wife who is reading a magazine in the living room. The caption reads, "Well, so much for the work ethic. Who wants to join me in a drink ethic?" I invite you in this chapter to think about these three comments on our current human condition.

If we have an urgent need to think more creatively about our self-definitions as *Homo faber* and *Homo ludens,* it might be fruitful to ask first if women and men have different understandings and experiences of work and play. Do we have grounds for different concepts of producing and playing? Thereafter, we will inquire about our common experiences of play and work, leisure and labor. For that dialectic in our experience of shared time is unquestionably a basic ingredient in any recipe for what it means to be human.

Let us go back once again to the primordial myths to ask about a necessary division of labor. Genesis 1 says no; as equally in the image of God, we share equally in the charge to have dominion over creation. Genesis 3 says yes; men will till the soil with sweat on their faces and women will writhe in childbirth. The dual meaning of our English word "labor" is redolent with pain.

Until recent years, the Genesis 3 version of male-female roles in the human economy dominated the surface of American thought, as it seems to have dominated biblical thought. Men produced bread; women produced children. Woman will be saved, according to the author of 1 Timothy, through bearing children. Apart from that major creative function, woman is often cast in the role of consumer, not producer. The relation between social injustice and conspicuous consumption was as well known to the prophet Amos in the eighth century B.C. as it is to our latter day prophets. Listen to his words to the women of Samaria:

> Hear this word, you cows of Bashan, who oppress the poor, who crush the needy, who say to their husbands, "Bring, that we may drink . . ."
>
> (Amos 4:2)

Writing in A.D. 1974 about the "validating activities" people must have to confirm their sense of themselves as fully active members of society, a Harvard University professor of sociology argued that women today validate themselves as good cooks. Husbands and fathers, he wrote, traditionally have had the role of provider. To the extent that they are able to bring home the resources which approximate "the mainstream package" they feel right about themselves. Wives and mothers have felt validated only to the extent that they can use that package to provide their families with "a mainstream existence" in the home. Currently, he said, a mainstream existence calls for meat on the table. If a wife is not able to feed her family meat with the money her husband provides, she will blame both her husband and herself.[1]

In our society the husband/father is still expected to be the provider, this sociologist claimed. That may well still be the expectation on the surface of our society's attitude toward the proper division of labor between men and women, but it is a social myth with very little connection either with economic facts or with the human saga. Historically, of course, women have always produced more than children and high-protein dinners. A story from the *Boston Evening News* of 1796 makes this point graphically clear. Praising the industry of "the wife of Mr. Stephen Rogers," it itemizes her day's accomplishments:

> . . . milk'd 8 cows in the morning—made her cheeses—turned and took care of fourscore cheeses—made a number of beds—swept her house, consisting of three rooms—spun six skeins of worsted yarn—baked a batch of bread—churned a quantity of butter—and milked 7 cows in the evening.[2]

(What do you suppose happened to that other cow?)

Women worked hard at home, but women also worked outside their homes from colonial days to the present. First they worked as slaves and servants; then, with industrialization, as factory workers; and then increasingly, as office workers, salesclerks, teachers. By 1890 one out of every six workers in the labor force (that is,

48

people working for pay) was female. By 1960, one out of three.[3] In the last twenty years the proportion has grown rapidly. It is sometimes argued that women work today because they are bored at home—that increased labor-saving devices and smaller families are responsible for the dramatic increase of women working in the marketplace. Studies show, on the contrary, that most women work because of economic necessity.

Nevertheless, in the ranks of full-time, year-round workers in 1971, women earned only sixty percent as much as men. In part this was true because they did not get equal pay for equal work. Chiefly it was because they were crowded into low-paying "female" occupations. Some interpreters think that cultural (for which read "male") discrimination is solely responsible for this disparity in income. Others recognize that American women have deeply internalized this cultural stereotyping so that they have low aspirations for themselves. Only seven percent of the physicians in the United States, just a few years ago, were women.

Clearly men and women have different experiences of the meaning of work in our society. Two additional dimensions of those different experiences seem to be of importance for theological reflection. First, there is some suggestion that women in the work force are less dissatisfied with their jobs than men. After reading Studs Terkel's *Working: People Talk About What They Do All Day and How They Feel About What They Do,* Seward Hiltner produced an article called, "Needed: A New Theology of Work." One of his comments, unelaborated, was that "perhaps it is not an accident" that most of the "gems" about work in these taped interviews with American workers came from women.[4] They were the ones who spoke more often and more eloquently of fulfillment in their work.

A second aspect of our different experiences is that for the male (until very recently at least) the principal source of his self-identification in society was through his work outside the home, whereas for the female there were often at least two and sometimes three human sources of her capacity to know the meaning of her life, to know who she was and why. She spoke of her identity in relation to husband and children, and outside employment, if any. The significance of a man's life was more explicitly linked to his experience in a context wider than the family. For a woman, per-

49

sonal significance tended to be measured by her relationship with a man and their children as well as by her "other work." The dual or multiple sources of self-identification and self-worth are not an unmixed blessing for women, but neither is the single source for men.

One of the most moving expressions of a women's struggle for identity that I have ever read is from the diary of the noted social anthropologist, Ruth Benedict. Her dilemma confirms what Sebastian de Grazia so well recognized in his landmark study *Of Time, Work and Leisure*—that a woman torn between home and career is worse off than an ass equidistant between two bales of hay.[5] As she moves toward one, the other recedes.

Benedict started her journal when she was still a young woman groping toward self-definition. The journal is pervaded by sadness because she lived in a time (or so she thought) when it was hard for love and useful work to coincide. Writing in 1912, while she was still teaching in a girls' school, and before she had discovered her "career," she said:

> So much of the trouble is because I am a woman. To me it seems a very terrible thing to be a woman. There is one crown which perhaps is worth it all—a great love, a quiet home and children. We all know that is all that is worthwhile . . . we have not the motive to prepare ourselves for a "life-work" of teaching, of social work—we know that we would lay it down with a hallelujah in the height of our success, to make a home for the right man.[6]

For a man, then and now, the situation is other but by no means better. He knows who he is primarily by being a plumber or a professor, a lobbyist or a lumberman—so the studies tell us. And yet, he gets only limited satisfaction from this work that tells him who he is. The evidence is overwhelming that the "work ethic" of America, if not dead, is very sick indeed.

And that brings us to our *second* cartoon from *The New Yorker*, picturing a psychiatrist's couch. The caption reads, "My Protestant work ethic made me a bundle, but my Puritan guilt complex wouldn't let me enjoy it." Only a ripple below the surface of this would-be funny line is the question of how we experience and evaluate time. In other words, the basic question is, why don't we ever say "Thank God, it's Monday!"?

First we must take time to lay to rest the ghost of Max Weber and come to the defense of the Puritans. At the same time we can pause to ask ouselves why we think (if, in fact, we do) that paid work is better than free play.

Weber's book, *The Protestant Ethic and the Spirit of Capitalism,* has had a great influence on our everyday language, as the cartoon caption shows; but the phrase, "Protestant work ethic" is used chiefly by those who have never read the book. First published in 1904, the book attracted and deserved wide critical attention. The title has unfortunately become a peg to hang our clichés on, totally divorced from Weber's argument. Just to set the historical record straight, we need to realize that what we sometimes call the Protestant work ethic is much older than Protestantism and also, in its American dress, much younger than classical Protestant ethics.

Weber himself recognized that the roots of what he called the "Protestant ethic" lie deep in monasticism. He did not argue, although others could, that St. Benedict is as much responsible for our attitudes toward time and work as John Calvin. If the Reformation helped make everyone a monk, as Weber claimed, that is another matter.

Weber also realized that our American "spirit of capitalism" can be most easily illustrated from the writings of Benjamin Franklin, whom he quotes at length. Weber calls Franklin "a colourless deist." He puts undue stress on the fact that Franklin had a Calvinist father and Puritan ancestors. Franklin himself was a post-Protestant.

When Ben Franklin wrote satirical articles under the pseudonym "Mrs. Silence Dogood," he was attacking, not reflecting Puritan theology. When Franklin listed frugality and industry among the virtues, he wrote as a Yankee moralist untroubled by thoughts of God. His text makes that clear:

5. Frugality—Make no expense but to do good to others or yourself; that is, waste nothing.
6. Industry—Lose no time; be always employed in something useful; cut off all unnecessary actions.[7]

An ungodly Puritan is no Puritan at all.

If Weber was right in his conclusion that the idea of duty in one's calling "prowls about in our lives like the ghost of dead re-

ligious beliefs,"[8] that ghost cannot fairly be labeled "Protestant."
The best of Franklin's Poor Richard sayings were collected under
the title *The Way to Wealth*. They represent a cut-flower moralism.

The contrast can be seen sharply if one turns to the idea of work
expressed when Puritanism was blooming. A Puritanism which was
at once a spiritual experience, a pattern of life, and a form of
expression informed the pen of that seventeenth-century working
tinker, John Bunyan:

> Since, Lord, thou dost defend
>   Us with thy Spirit,
> We know we at the end
>   Shall life inherit.
> Then fancies flee away!
> I'll fear not what men say,
> I'll labor night and day,
>   To be a Pilgrim.

When English Puritanism moved to America, furthermore, forests had to be cleared and crops planted. In the first generation,
at least, everyone worked continually and concertedly. As Herbert
Wallace Schneider sagely observes, "Not even Puritans worked
merely for the love of it; they worked of necessity."[9] And they
rested from their daily labor every seventh day to give glory to
God. Only in later generations was the Puritan idea of the glory
of God reduced to a moral concept.

It was prosperous, commercial Yankees who discarded the Puritan dependence on God and turned religion into "Americanism."
The naked end product is visible in Richard Nixon's words:

> The "work ethic" holds that labor is good in itself; that a man or
> woman becomes a better person by virtue of the act of working.
> America's competitive spirit, the "work ethic" of this people, is alive
> and well on Labor Day, 1971.[10]

This comes frighteningly close to the perverted work-idolatry bru-
tally inscribed over the only gate into Dachau: *Arbeit macht frei*—
"work makes us free."

The Western march toward the work society, we said earlier,
may well have begun in the monastery, especially a Benedictine
monastery. The Rule of St. Benedict, written in the early sixth
century, directed that "at fixed times" the brothers should be en-

gaged in manual labor (it notes that the apostles before them had worked with their hands), and at other "fixed times" in sacred reading. But the celebration of the divine office at the canonical hours was the monk's first duty. No other demand on his time took precedence.

Commenting on the rule, Sebastian de Grazia links it to our modern habits of living by the clock. Do you remember that old round of your childhood, "Frère Jacques"? Are you sleeping, Brother John? To monks such as Frère Jacques, de Grazia contends (without contest), the bed felt good in the cold, early morning. "So bells and clocks were used as never before to pull monks out of bed, to send them off to prayers, and then to the fields, to mark off time for work and prayer and contemplation."[11]

Fine and good, but I do not think that our modern fixation on hours and minutes can be blamed on the Benedictines any more than our current ideas of a work ethic can be charged against the Puritans. The Benedictine Rule, de Grazia implies, led straight to what is now called Taylorism. This -ism is named after the major proponent of Time/Work/Efficiency studies. A person with a stopwatch in hand stood behind you at work and determined how many tenths of a second were needed to tighten that screw. The atomization of time had reached its ultimate end. *

Taylorism is now generally repudiated by responsible students of work in America in favor of growing concern over the quality of life which revised working conditions can promote. But from its inception Taylorism suffered from a double built-in fault. It subscribed to the thesis that time is money. And it failed to recognize that, as human subjects, "workers" have a different perception from stopwatches of what time is.

What appears to be alive and well in America today is neither Taylorism nor the work ethic Nixon advocated, but two other approaches to time and work. One looks on work as a way of making money to buy free time in which to do something else. The other looks on work as an opportunity for pleasure and self-fulfillment. Dorothy L. Sayers noted these basically different attitudes in a talk she once gave on the BBC, a talk called "Living to Work."[12] They have popped up again in the interviews recorded in Studs Terkel's *Working*.

* According to Rubin, time is often best spent when we are "wasting" time in the eyes of the productive economy for it is then that time passes with more perceived moderation; it does not seem to run by beyond our grasp or control.

53

It is easy to scoff in a simplistic way at the idea of working for money. The dollar value on work is deeply connected with our sense of personal worth. If we do a job we expect to be paid for it, not necessarily because we need the money, but because that payment acknowledges that our work was worthwhile in the eyes of the other. (The obverse of this is the American conviction that you don't get something for nothing; patients have less respect for "free clinics" than for those in which they pay even a modest fee.) As countless women know, there is a stigma attached to what is called "volunteer work," in spite of all the service done for others through thousands of hours donated that way. Working for money is not the real issue here. Rather, it is working just to "make a living," with the clear implication that real life begins when the work hours are over. This is the "Thank God, it's Friday!" philosophy.

The other attitude toward work is related to "having a good time." Some people enjoy what they are doing at work. They find room in their jobs for individual initiative, for social relationships, for a satisfying sense of contributing to society. And such experiences are by no means limited to those in what are today called the helping professions, nor to artists or self-employed artisans. In the light of the evidence that jobs fulfill human needs, one economist commented, "An hour of work may well be more enjoyable than an hour of leisure."[13] In such a situation, a person may well say, "Thank God, it's Monday!"

What does all of this tell us about the nature of human beings in theological perspective? Partly, of course, that work itself is in need of redemption. And partly as well that we cannot simply return to the days of John Bunyan's brand of Calvinism to solve the complicated problems of American workers in the year 2000. As Hiltner remarked, John Calvin "never had to express an opinion about moving the work week for local 3104 from 36 to 32 hours."[14] But beyond that, it points, I think, to our common human experience of the polarities of slavery and freedom, of work and play, in such a way that we need to emphasize more strongly both rhythms of our life in time.

For help in that direction, I summon my *third* cartoon from *The New Yorker*, the one in which a man says to his wife, "Well, so much for the work ethic. Who wants to join me in a drink ethic?" A man returning from work asks a question about refreshment. Since he undoubtedly was not thinking about Coca-Cola, we do not have to think just about a pause before going back to work. And since he attaches the word "ethic," we are permitted to think seriously about happy hours in our lives together. The growing literature on leisure recognizes that leisure has three essential elements: renouncement of work, play, and solitude. In classical times, leisure meant just the last of these. The philosopher Seneca, for example, writing on leisure, *De otio,* urges that a person devote life wholly to the contemplation of truth. From earliest years one should search out the art of living and practice it "in retirement." The ever-changing meanings of words are with us again. By retirement, Seneca meant a young man getting away from public busyness. "Otiose" in English now means futile. Solitude and contemplation will concern us later, however. We are currently thinking about the social aspects of leisure.

Renouncement of work and recovery of play are matters of tremendous importance to contemporary society. They are also matters on which biblical thought can shed a great deal of light. The topics are separable, but not separate.

To renounce work implies the right to be lazy. It suggests that it is good to do nothing, just to be. To lie back against a tree trunk, put your arms behind your head, and look about you. Or to close your eyes and take a nap, as Jesus did on a cushion in the stern of a boat (Mark 4:38). Bertrand Russell once wrote an essay "In Praise of Idleness," proposing a four-hour work day so that we might devote the other twenty hours to enjoyment.

Renouncing work means resting. According to the biblical understanding of human being, we need to spend one full day out of every seven just resting. That, at least, is one dominant theme in the traditions of the sabbath. At all levels of the tradition, God's command to Israel is to stop working; but different rationales are given for why this should occur once a week.

The Priestly version of the Ten Commandments says that we should rest because God himself rests:

> Six days you shall labor, and do all your work; but the seventh day is a sabbath to the Lord your God; in it you shall not do any work

55

... for in six days the Lord made heaven and earth, the sea, and all that is in them, and rested the seventh day; therefore the Lord blessed the sabbath day and hallowed it.

(Exod. 20:9–11)

A later passage expands on the nature of God's rest. The sabbath is a sign forever between God and his people. It is a day of solemn rest because on the seventh day the Lord "rested and was refreshed." (Exod. 31:17) Both passages point back, of course, to the climax of the earlier narrative in which we are said to be made in the image of God. The Jerusalem Bible similarly indicates that God might have been tired:

On the seventh day God completed the work he had been doing. He rested on the seventh day after all the work he had been doing. God blessed the seventh day and made it holy, because on that day he had rested after all his work of creating.

(Gen. 2:1–2)

Can we today make any sense out of the anthropomorphic notion that creating is exhausting work even for God? Hans Walter Wolff suggests that the emphasis is on God's finished work, and that we cannot find a right relationship either to our work or to our rest without that focus.[15]

This insight points directly to the Christian understanding that our work is not going to save either ourselves or the world. God has already done that in his finished work on the cross. Presupposing a unity in biblical thought about God's work in creation and re-creation, God's weariness here reminds one of the conversation that the prophet Isaiah had with King Ahaz about his lack of trust in the Lord: "Is it too little for you to weary men, that you weary my God also?" (Isa. 7:13). Or again of the promised gift of rest that God will give to those who toil and are heavy laden—through his own self-giving (Matt. 11:28).

The themes of God's work and God's rest pervade the New Testament as well as the Old, in counterpoint with the themes of human rest and human labor. The author of Hebrews meditates directly on Gen. 2:2 to conclude that there remains a sabbath rest for the people of God, "for whoever enters God's rest also ceases from his labors as God did from his" (Heb. 4:10).

The Priestly document itself, however, clearly sees the sense-

56 * *How many times have we worked hard to fix something up or finish something only to fail to take the time to enjoy it, to sit back and actually see it finished.*

lessness of uninterrupted work. The manna from heaven story dramatizes this senselessness with a touch of humor. When the Israelites were in the wilderness, God gave them bread every day. But on the sixth day he gave them enough for two days, so that they would not have to go out to work the next morning. Even so, some people went out to look for bread on that morning, too, just as they did every other day. But, the narrative says "they found none" (Exod. 16:27). Apparently, workaholics are not a new thing on the face of the earth.

What this interpretation of the sabbath emphasizes is the gift character of freedom from work. The Israelite community on its weekly sabbath could acknowledge that God creates time and controls it. Therefore they were freed from its ceaseless demands.

A second explicit Old Testament rationale for keeping the sabbath, in the other version of the Decalogue, relates that day to freedom in another sense. The community is to stop working in order to remember that they were once slaves. Their present liberty is the gift of God.

> Six days you shall labor, and do all your work; but the seventh day is a sabbath to the Lord your God; in it you shall not do any work . . . You shall remember that you were a servant in the land of Egypt, and the Lord your God brought you out. . . .
>
> (Deut. 5:13–15)

Again we have the stark contrast between working and not working, but now we are not meant only to rest. We are to remember our previous bondage to work and God's initiative in delivering us from slave labor. So stop slaving away. Take time to remember that God is the author of your right to leisure as well as the author of your right to work. He created and he remains sovereign over both of our time experiences.

In this Deuteronomic account of the sabbath, then, we have the basis not just of sabbath rest, but of sabbath joy. That one day out of seven is a festival, a time of celebration, a time of play. From this perspective, every Jewish sabbath is a time for remembering *the exodus*. The first response to God's great act of liberation, according to the Bible, was singing and dancing—led by Miriam and all the women with her (Exod. 15:20).

With Christian reshuffling of time, every Sunday is an Easter,

57

a time for celebrating Christ's resurrection from the dead and his new gift of freedom. And with this shift the time for celebration starts the week instead of ending it. For it was on the first day of the week that "Mary Magdalene and Joanna and Mary the mother of James and the other women with them" went at early dawn and learned the good news (Luke 24:10).

It is hard for some Christians to think of Sunday as essentially a day of play. We are victims of a Sabbatarian heritage which confused Sunday with Saturday, and misunderstood Saturday to boot. Under that weight, Sunday became the dullest day of the week. Our desire to turn gift into duty is endemic. The story of how the day of liberation was turned into a day of inhibition is another chapter in the story of our distorting the image of God.

The gospels record a great deal of controversy between Jesus and his fellow Jews about the meaning of the Sabbath. Indeed, his free behavior on that day, it is said, was one of the principal causes of his arrest. But even though Jesus picked grain on the seventh day, and healed crippled women and blind men, he did not repudiate the Sabbath. Instead he went into synagogues and taught. One of his well-attested teachings is that the Sabbath was made for human beings, not human beings for the Sabbath (Mark 2:27, *anthrōpōs*).

Jesus' power to reverse normal ways of looking at things liberates us to think about recurring cycles of play. We have difficulty with the whole notion of adults playing. That is the prerogative of puppies, kittens, and small children. We turn adult play into *dis*-play, as any viewer of what we call sports can see nightly on prime time television.

The renewed interest in a theology of play a few years ago, however, helped us to rediscover that play is one mode of authentic selfhood. If we continue to play, we can continue becoming fully human. We need both the Apollonian and the Dionysian ways. We need both Tom Sawyer and Ben Rogers.

Look at Tom Sawyer whitewashing the fence on that unforgettable Saturday morning. Thanks to Aunt Polly, he is, reluctantly but unmistakably, Man at Work. But down the street, thanks to Mark Twain and Robert Neale, comes Man at Play. It is Ben Rogers. No, it is the steamboat "Big Missouri." Ben Rogers is absorbed

58

in make-believe. He is wrapped up in the mystery "which throws the meaning and hope of the everyday world into question."[16]

Robert Neale recognized in Ben Rogers the sense of freedom and of peace which play brings, and the spirit of adventure it demands, a spirit which always involves risk and openness to change. That is why Ben could so quickly turn from being "The Big Missouri" into being the "Glorious Whitewasher," and even spend his apple core for the privilege.

Sam Keen's apologia for a Dionysian theology draws a comparable contrast.[17] The Apollonian way, which has dominated American life and American religious thought too long, stresses human beings as makers, fabricators, molders, and manipulators of the environment. We order our experience. We make the will and the intellect central. We put high value on work, on action.

The Dionysian way stresses the dancer, responding to the givenness of life, recognizing its diversity and vitality. It makes feeling and sensation central. It puts high value on leisure, on play. It bursts the boundaries of the average way.

Insofar as we have lost the faculty of play, forgotten how to be Ben Rogers or Dionysus, that Greek god of wine and revelry, we have become beings without mystery, shriveling our lives. We need to learn again to play the games of freedom.

A long tradition of Christian thought has spoken of the creation not as God's work but as God's play. This interpretation stems from the Greek text (LXX) of Prov. 8:30–31, which called the Father's cocreator a child at play. That text led to Christian portraits of the Christ child holding, even tossing, the globe of the world like a ball in his hand. Speaking out on behalf of this tradition, Hugo Rahner parallels the playing of God with the playing of human beings.

Human beings should be players, he says, people who in all their manifold activities imitate as fully as possible God's own creative power by lightness of touch and regard for beauty. As we play, we learn that our lives are joyous and free because they are secure in God. But if we truly play, we will also be profoundly serious, seeking to synthesize our laughter and our tears.

Our challenge is to journey between frivolity and despair, Friday and Monday, conscious of a tremendous secret. According to Rah-

59

ner, when we contemplate the creative play of God we discover that all play is an attempt to be "approximate to the Creator," and the Creator is one who accomplishes his work not only with divine seriousness but also with spontaneity. God is creating "because he wills to create and not because he must."[18]

Playtime is every bit as important as worktime in our growing up to be fully human. Our self images need to reflect not only what we make and build and do, but also how we remake and rebuild and are. Creation and recreation are both essential ingredients in our social lives together. But in our day recreation deserves stronger applause than our ancestors St. Benedict or John Calvin or John Bunyan or Ben Franklin gave it. The mutual interchange of energy between our modes of "spending" time deserves our Amen! For human beings who start their week in a spirit of playfulness, working days take on more of the character of play, too. The community at play is also in the image of God.

NOTES

1. Lee Rainwater, "Work, Well-Being and Family Life," in James O'Toole, ed., *Work and the Quality of Life* (Cambridge, Mass.: MIT Press, 1974), p. 364.

2. As quoted by Harold D. Lehman, *In Praise of Leisure* (Scottsdale, Pa.: Herald Press, 1974), p. 93.

3. Isabel V. Sawhill, "Perspectives on Women and Work in America," in O'Toole, *Work and the Quality of Life,* p. 90.

4. Seward Hiltner, "Needed: A New Theology of Work," *Theology Today* 31 (1974): 244.

5. Sebastian de Grazia, *Of Time, Work and Leisure* (New York: Doubleday & Co., 1964), p. 244.

6. Mary Jane Moffat and Charlotte Painter, eds., *Revelations: Diaries of Women* (New York: Random House, 1974), p. 150.

7. Benjamin Franklin, *Autobiography,* as quoted by Herbert Wallace Schneider, *The Puritan Mind* (Ann Arbor, Mich.: University of Michigan Press, 1958), p. 243.

8. Max Weber, *The Protestant Ethic and the Spirit of Capitalism* (New York: Charles Scribner's Sons, 1958), p. 182.

9. Schneider, *The Puritan Mind,* p. 81.

10. Cited by Susan Jacoby, "Not by Bread Alone," *Sr/World* (April 20, 1974): 26.

11. de Grazia, *Of Time,* p. 40.

12. Dorothy L. Sayers, *Unpopular Opinions* (London: Victor Gollancz, 1946), pp. 122–127.

13. Lester Thurow, "The American Economy in the Year 2000," *American Economic Review* 62 (1972): 442, as cited by Sawhill, "Perspectives on Women," p. 89.

14. Hiltner, "New Theology of Work," p. 246.

15. Hans Walter Wolff, *Anthropology of the Old Testament* (Philadelphia: Fortress Press, 1974), p. 138.

16. Robert Neale, "The New Leisure and the Glorious Whitewasher," *Union Seminary Quarterly Review* 21 (1966): 449–456.

17. Sam Keen, *Apology for Wonder* (New York: Harper & Row, 1969), Chapter 6.

18. Hugo Rahner, *Man at Play* (London: Burns and Oates, 1965), p. 26 ff.

PART II

Each With a Name

CHAPTER FIVE

Embodied Selves

Human life is lived in the first person plural. I cannot even become a person unless I am related to other persons, unless I am a social being. Yet, social being that I am, I also live my life in the first person singular. I am an "I" as well as a "Thou." And as an "I," I am necessarily related to myself. I am made to be lonely. In this second section of reflections on what it means to be human, we will address this singular dimension of creaturehood.

The question "Who am I?" haunts many of us in the dark of night and in line at the supermarket. We can buy answers to our question by the dozen from the paperback racks in our airports, and think about them for credit at any community college. Does Christian theology have any special insight toward an answer, any reasonable working hypothesis to exchange for dreams of immortality or for life on the streets?

Those seem to be the chief alternatives presented to us in the classic literature of the Western world. From Wolfgang von Goethe through Tennessee Williams, we are asked to believe that men like to sell their souls and that women like to sell their bodies. But, in Christian perspective, no such half-breed is on the market.

Giving up our immortal souls is hard for most of us. We are fond of the notion inherited from Plato that something within us cannot be killed, that our soul is our true self, our guarantee of eternal life. But, if Christians are right, we are deluding ourselves.

Lifting our bodies to any status beyond that of a temporary prison house or a source of pain and embarrassment is equally threatening. We can jog them around the block, make them do sit-ups, or put them on a diet, but they are not "us." We do not like being incarnate.

In opposition to our literary tradition and our personal predi-lections, Christian theology affirms our psycho-physical unity, our integrity as embodied selves. It recognizes that each of us has a rich potential for strong and compassionate selfhood, transcending any cultural stereotypes of what is "feminine" and what is "mas-culine." And our theology celebrates the unique personhood of each and every being by giving us a Christian name. These three themes—*incarnation, wholeness, and uniqueness*—need our attention.

Christian tradition at many times and in many places has failed to do justice to all three of these consequences of our faith in Jesus Christ. A quick reading of Christian history leaves the impression that we are dualists who favor a one-sided development of our personalities and masochism for half of our number. As we con-sider these three aspects of our human individuality, we must look at this negative side of our Christian heritage. We have a lot to unlearn. But brainwashing need not always have sinister conno-tations.

One of the great ironies of the history of Christian thought is that the two thinkers who probably did more than anyone else to contribute to dualistic misunderstanding of ourselves were St. Paul and St. Augustine, whereas consciously both of them were fighting *against* dualistic religious outlooks on the nature of human beings. Because of their writings, we have for centuries been led to think that we are souls inhabiting bodies, like tenants in low-income housing.

In the name of Christ, St. Paul, as we said earlier, was combating a bifurcated view of reality which led people to hope for rescue from their imprisonment in the flesh. The Hellenistic world of his day contrasted the soul—"the invisible, spiritual, essential ego"[1]—with the girders of matter in which it was incarcerated. It offered a way of liberation from the grubby facts of physical existence by imparting a secret wisdom or gnosis, letting you know that the real

65

you has nothing to do with your body. An ancient injunction to the "pneumatic man" of a Hellenistic mystery religion, to the spiritual being who knows himself, offers a clear example of such an attitude:

> Seeking only himself and having known God, let him hold fast the nameless triad, and let fate do what it wishes to do with his clay, that is, the body.[2]

Any reader of the New Testament could easily conclude that St. Paul fully shared this attitude toward our clay. A passage from his letter to the Romans, for example, seems to express a totally negative evaluation of our embodied condition. He is saying that he does not understand his own actions:

> So then it is no longer I that do it, but sin which dwells within me. For I know that nothing good dwells within me, that is, in my flesh.

> (Rom. 7:17–18)

How can any casual reader fail to think that Paul considered his flesh to be the seat of sin, just as the gnostic writer thought that the body was not truly himself, especially if one reads this passage along with Paul's many warnings against walking "according to the flesh"?

Biblical scholars in our day have done a great deal to liberate us from a gnostic reading of Paul's idea of human being. They have effectively retranslated his letters so as to render a more accurate English translation of what Paul actually says in Greek. The most dramatic and, in theological perspective, the soundest change has been the translation of *psychē*.

Although *psychē* is not one of the major terms in Paul's anthropological vocabulary, it is an important one in ours. To recognize that we are not disembodied souls, and that St. Paul did not believe that we are, is of utmost significance for our Christian understanding of what it means to be human. So it is a major step forward to learn that when, according to the seventeenth-century translators, Paul wrote, "there will be tribulation and distress for every soul that does evil" (KJV Rom. 2:9), he really meant "for every human being," as both the Revised Standard Version and the Jerusalem Bible claim.

Paul, that is, was not operating primarily out of Greek categories when he talked about an apparent opposition between soul and body, flesh and spirit. Rather, as J.A.T. Robinson argued long ago, his fundamental anthropological ideas were Hebraic. He shared the Hebrew belief that human being is "flesh-animated-by-soul, the whole conceived as a psycho-physical unity."[3] And thus, in such passages as the one we cited from Romans 7, the category of flesh *(sarx)* is not to be equated simply with the material realm. Rather, "flesh" means just human beings living *in* the world (and in this sense it is a neutral term). "Flesh" becomes a negative term when it is used of human beings living *for* the world.[4]

That "flesh" is not simply physical in Paul's mind becomes eminently clear when in his letter to the Galatians he contrasts the desires of the flesh with the fruit of the spirit. "Anger" and "party spirit," for example, are listed in the former category; "patience" and "gentleness" in the latter (Gal. 5:19–23). Can you imagine "gentleness" without some physical expression or "anger" without some connection with your spirit?

In his discussions of Paul's anthropology, Rudolf Bultmann reached similar conclusions about the meaning of the Pauline vocabulary. Paul is always talking, Bultmann says, about the concrete, embodied person in relation to God. His dualistic language is not finally the language of metaphysical dualism, although it is influenced by such attractive speculations. Our flesh and our mind or inner self are not two separate entities which together make up one person. Instead, Paul is talking about "the total tendency of human existence."[5] We are empirical selves, that is, *incarnate* psycho-physical unities, who are concerned about our true natures and who find our true natures only when we orient our total selves toward God.

As a young man living in North Africa in the fourth century, St. Augustine was also seeking to understand himself and his world. So, when he was in his twenties, he became a Manichean—a devotee of an eclectic Indo-Iranian religion which was as popular among young people then as the teachings of some Eastern religious movements are among young people today. Augustine remained a Manichean for nine years.

Mani, the founder of the religion, has been called the last of the great gnostics. The religion he founded was missionary-minded, and it spread far and wide, East and West, in the third and fourth centuries. Like Paul's opponents at Corinth, Mani taught contempt for our material existence—and a means of escape from its horrors. He believed that the material body was formed by the powers of evil, whereas the human soul or spirit represented God-like light imprisoned in the darkness of the flesh. The goal for the followers of Mani was redemption of the soul from the body.

In his *Confessions* Augustine tells us why for so long he could not accept the Christian claim that Jesus the Christ was God made known in the flesh. The Savior, he thought, could not be born of the Virgin Mary "without being mingled with the flesh . . . I feared therefore to believe Him born in the flesh, lest I should be forced therefore to believe Him defiled by the flesh."[6]

Although when he wrote that the Christian Augustine was smiling on his youthful stupidity, many of his modern readers, with good reason, think that Augustine never fully outgrew the dualistic conceptions of his Manichean past. Intellectually he discovered the weaknesses of the Manichean position and wrote at length against it. But he continued to think of a body-soul dichotomy in ways that down-graded the body. Augustine's contributions to our thinking about individual selfhood lie in other areas, as we shall see.

Looking in a mirror can be a healthy antidote to Gnosticism, to that divorce of flesh and spirit which has so plagued Christian thought from Paul's time to our own. What I see there as "me" is so essentially a bonding of the two that selfhood actually defines what Christian theology means by the adjective "sacramental." My physical reality is both the matrix and the communicator of my psychic life. I do not have a body; *I am one.* I do not have a soul or *psychē; I am one.* "I" come into being and live and grow in the process we call life, in the inextricable interconnection of matter and spirit.

The immense mystery of being who we are is reflected from that looking glass. "I" know and affirm that this aging person with gray hair is the same "me" that once looked into the mirror at a missing front tooth when I was six. I know that all the experiences I have had in the interim, dental and otherwise, have made me different but not other. Looking into a mirror confirms what we said earlier about a person being an event and not a thing. My experience of the continuity of myself is an experience of movement in time, an experience of who I am today, en route to whom I may become tomorrow. But my yesterdays come with me.

The self that I recognize in my bathroom mirror as I brush my teeth today is a female self. For most of us self-perception includes our sense of gender-identity. If we affirm selfhood as a sacramental reality, we need to ask how our self-understandings as male and female human beings affect our individual lives. We need to talk with Carl Jung.

In recent years many Christian theologians have discovered creative resources for a new appreciation of human nature in the theories of that noted depth psychologist. Some, indeed, seem to find in Jungian thought the answer to all of our perplexities about what it means to be a unique human self. I agree that he offered Christian thinkers bright spotlights on who we are individually. Yet I find it necessary to raise a serious question about the adequacy of his idiom for discussing what it means to be a person in the image of God.

Our *uniqueness* as human beings was of primary concern for the Swiss psychiatrist—a fact that is often obscured by popular accounts of his basic theories. His long-time friend, Laurens van der Post, has conveyed well this emphasis on our distinctiveness. For Jung, the South African writer says, "isms" (including Jungianism) were like viruses, infections to be fought. What Jung most wanted was for people to be themselves. He had a profound recognition that each of us has our own story clamoring to be lived.[7] We cannot be reduced even to the story of our collective unconsciousness.

One interpreter of Jung found that his writings really contain two concepts of the self.[8] The first concept is simply of the self as the totality of the human psyche at present—conscious and unconscious. This idea of the self strengthens the sense of embodied personhood we have just considered. My "inscape"—to use Gerard Manley Hopkins's phrase—and my "landscape" have a reciprocal relationship. My subjective experience is rooted in my objective experience "out there"—and vice versa. As van der Post says of his own experience, "The relationships between spirit and matter, world within and world without, are transcendental and incapable of total expression in non-transcendental terms. . . . I never

69

doubted that the physical world is spirit seen from without and the spirit is world viewed from within."[9]

Jung's other view of the self demands a capital letter. The Self is the *goal* of psychic development, the realization of one's potential. This is what individuation means. And from this teleological perspective in Jungian thought, "God" is the symbol of the Self as goal. The *imago dei* constitutes, as it were, a version of Jesus' saying that we must become fully mature, fully grown-up, just as our Father in heaven is (cf. Matt. 5:48). When a person understands that talk about God is really talk about the Self, according to this interpretation of Jung, that person is set free on the path toward individuation. He or she is ready to explore "that unfathomable expanse of mystery and continual wonder which envelops the waking subject like a vast uncharted ocean."[10]

Without accepting the conclusion that "God" is simply a synonym for self with that capital "S," we can nonetheless agree that Jung's concept of individuation helps us form a dynamic concept of what it means to become a person. I am in the process of becoming me, that unique individual I am created to be. And the process requires a lifetime. My "self" is by no means a finished product, even though I may be past the half-century mark.

Ann Belford Ulanov thinks that Jung's description of the ongoing phase of individuation is his main contribution to developmental psychology. As she charts the process, becoming whole demands "realization of our innermost uniqueness," a uniqueness which distinguishes each of us from our various collective identities such as race, nation, or profession. It is a process by which a person becomes, in Jung's words, "a psychological 'in-dividual,' that is, a separate, indivisible unity or 'whole.'" Individuation must be distinguished from individualism, however. A truly individuated person does not shut out the world but "gathers the world to oneself."[11]

A third major insight which Jungian thought offers to the reflective Christian, in addition to emphasis on our uniqueness and on the process of growth, is perhaps the best known—that is, the recognition of our "contrasexuality." Each male has within him, Jungians say, an *anima* of feminine gender. Each female has within her an *animus* of masculine gender. The challenge to human wholeness is to achieve a marriage between the two dimensions of our psyches—the one more conscious, the other less so.

Ulanov explains the Jungian idea of contrasexuality with admirable clarity. "The whole person for Jung is the contrasexual person, who is consciously related to internal male and female elements which operate in polarity to each other. . . . Masculine and feminine elements exist only in relation to each other and complement rather than fight each other. Feminine and masculine, then, are archetypal principles of the human psyche. . . ."[12]

Our culture has taught men to repress their "feminine" dimensions and women their "masculine" dimensions. It is liberating to discover that we do not have to be bound in our psychic development by cultural stereotyping. But, if we accept the notion that there are eternal archetypes corresponding to Jung's notions of Masculine and Feminine, are we not just perpetuating those cultural roles? To call nurturing qualities "feminine," for example, may not help a man to affirm those qualities in himself. And, similarly, to call rational thought "masculine" may not help a woman affirm her logical abilities. It is a serious question, I think, whether Jung—at least in popularized form—can really help us to move away from sexual polarization to full acceptance of all the polarities of our own individuality.

Defenders of Jung believe that he was able to transcend the ideas of masculine and feminine derived from his Swiss environment in the early years of the century. As one of them expressed it, "his genius was that he soared above these stereotypes in his search for the archetypal Masculine and Feminine."[13] Perhaps so. But the mythological bases for these archetypes appear to be found chiefly in Gnosticism, alchemy, astrology, and other esoteric traditions, as well as in Taoism.

The Jungian analyst, June Singer, has recently linked the dualities from such mythological traditions with contemporary research on the two hemispheres of the human brain.[14] A great body of evidence seems to suggest that there are, in fact, two complementary modes of human consciousness which are connected with the two sides of every human brain. It is widely agreed that Western culture has emphasized the mode of consciousness associated with the left hemisphere—intellectual, verbal, analytic capacities. The

*Jung, too, is so heavily influenced by the way things have been that he assumes they have to be that way in terms of gender identity.

right side appears to be associated more with such capacities as intuition, interpretation, musical skill. The first mode of consciousness is symbolized mythologically by day, the second by night. If everyone has such a brain, is there any basis for calling one mode of consciousness, the daytime one, "masculine," and the other, the nighttime one, "feminine?"

Or, to pose the same question in a different form, when Jesus wept, when he put a child in his lap, when he yearned to gather Jerusalem as a hen gathers her brood under her wings, was he being "feminine"? I think not. When he threw the money changers out of the temple and commanded the sick to rise up and walk, was he being "masculine"? I think not. Nor do I think he was being androgynous. Instead, I think he was being fully human, fully mature.

To be a fully human individual, as Jesus demonstrates what that means, requires enfleshment *(incarnation)* and compassionate selfhood. *It also requires a name.* The gospel tradition puts strong emphasis on the name "Jesus." In Matthew, Joseph learns in a dream what the child's name is to be. In Luke, Mary learns directly from the angel Gabriel that her son's name is to be Jesus. In both narratives the dramatic stress is on the meaning of the name Jesus. "Yahweh is salvation," but at the same time the stories reveal that a name is intimately connected with one's unique selfhood.

In biblical thought personal names are believed to have great significance and power. For the Hebrews names were practically identical with the essential nature of a person. Character and personality were conveyed by naming. To change a name signified a change of character, as when Jacob was renamed Israel (Gen. 32:28). The New Testament retains this idea that a change of character almost necessitates a change of name, as the switch from Saul of Tarsus to Paul, following his conversion, indicates.

Remembering a name is closely akin to sustaining life itself, in the Hebraic view. "One makes a name alive by remembering it," Johannes Pedersen once said, "the name immediately calls forth the soul it designates."[15] In time of trouble, Moses beseeches the Lord to remember Abraham, Isaac, and Israel, his servants (Exod. 32:13). Before he was killed, Absalom set up a monument to himself because, he said, "I have no son to keep my name in remembrance" (2 Sam. 18:18).

72

Conversely, forgetting a name is closely related to death. This is especially clear in the Psalms. "Come, let us wipe them out as a nation; let the name of Israel be remembered no more!" (83:4). Or again, "The face of the Lord is against evildoers, to cut off the remembrance of them from the earth" (34:16). One of the psalms of lament asks God that one's enemies may be "blotted out of the book of the living" (69:28).

That idea that individual human names are written in a heavenly book grew in popularity in the intertestamental period and made its way into the New Testament. There it is more, I think, than a picturesque piece of apocalyptic imagery. In St. Luke's gospel, Jesus tells the seventy to rejoice "that your names are written in heaven" (10:20). Paul says in his letter to the Philippians that the names of the women and men who have labored side by side with him "are in the book of life" (4:3). The same idea of names in a book recurs six times in the book of Revelation—in close association with witnessing to the name of Jesus (for example, Rev. 3:5). By this time, the idea clearly carries a heavy dose of determinism with it. The names were written there "before the foundation of the world" (13:8). But it is also clear that this is now "the book of the Lamb," and the names in it belong to those who bear on their foreheads not the mark of the beast but of the one who was slain. We are reminded that Jesus, according to the Fourth Gospel, is the shepherd who calls his own sheep by name (John 10:3). We are reminded that in baptism we are signed on the forehead with the sign of his cross.

In the development of Christian practice of baptism a twofold change occurred in relation to the bearing of a name. The New Testament evidence suggests that the earliest practice in Christian initiation was to baptize in the name of the Lord Jesus.[16] With the development of the doctrine of the Trinity came the elaboration of the baptismal formula, so that the candidates were baptized "in the name of the Father and of the Son and of the Holy Spirit," as St. Matthew's gospel directs (28:19).

As long as most people were adults at the time of baptism, there was no thought that this was an occasion for receiving one's own personal name, although a new and "indelible character" was later thought to be imparted by that rite in which the power of the divine name was invoked. The practice of converts taking a "Chris-

73

tian" name at baptism can be traced back only to the third century.

Gradually, however, as infant baptism became the norm in the Western church, the idea developed that this was the occasion for receiving one's own name and hence one's own identity as "a child of God and an inheritor of the kingdom of heaven." Thus, until recently, in the Book of Common Prayer, for example, the minister was to say to the godparents, "Name this child." The first two questions in the older catechism were "What is your name?" and "Who gave you this name?" The answer to be memorized was, "My Sponsors in Baptism . . . " Thus the child was encouraged to think of his or her self-identity having started with the new birth in Christ. In the older rite for thanksgiving after childbirth the child was still anonymous.

In post-Christian society, of course, a child's name goes on the birth certificate before the mother leaves the hospital. Parish records are no longer the official list of who's who in the community or in the kingdom of heaven. Contemporary baptismal rites accordingly no longer emphasize the Christian aspect of a given name. Indeed, a new rite of thanksgiving for the birth of a child, to be used "as soon as convenient" after the birth, requires that the child be named by name, whether the child has been baptized or not.

While these changes reflect secular practice and historical precedent, they also reflect profound theological and psychological realities. The biblical metaphors telling me that God knows my name affirm the radical particularity of his love for each and every human creature. The God who does not forget even one sparrow puts high value on the persons he remembers by name (cf. Luke 12:6–7). If I am nameless, or if I have forgotten who I am, I am unable to be myself and to function as a full member of society.

Christian ascetic theology, following the Negative Way, has often stressed giving up one's name as a symbol of renunciation of self. Thus the practice in monastic tradition has been to give up one's old name "in the world" and to take a new one, along with taking the vows of celibacy, chastity, and obedience. This practice perpetuates the ancient biblical notion of a new name coinciding with a new status and relationship.

If what I have said about the close interconnection between

74 ✳ This is yet the practice with Popes, but our present one is by far the most public and has a strong sense of self. Jesus was not totally public or private. He did both and Gandhi was probably much like him in being alone and with people.

names and selfhood has any validity, however, such a renunciation of identity is fraught with dangers. Although there is a possibility of profound redemptive power in the way of resignation, it can also become the way of the victim. One can just go limp and allow oneself to be carried downstream with the current. The way of resignation can indeed lead to neurosis and insanity. In her book *Women and Madness*,[17] Phyllis Chesler documented the extent to which a "be it unto me according to thy will" attitude can destroy selfhood.

Do you remember that almost-anonymous woman whose work-day, beginning and ending with milking cows, was reported in the last chapter? She was identified simply as "the wife of Mr. Stephen Rogers." In the early part of this century, a prominent American clergyman, Lyman Abbott, wrote a book which was apparently as widely read as a popular bridebook might be today. His prescription for the Christian bride was:

> She wishes a sovereign and is glad to have found him—no! to have been found by him. . . . To give up her home, abandon her name, merge her personality in his keeping—this is her glad ambition, and it swallows up all other ambitions.[18]

Can there be any graver misreading of our cohumanity in the image of God?

I have now claimed that, in Christian perspective, we are created not as no-body but as some-body. I have suggested that whatever our personal production of androgens and estrogens, each of us has the brain and the heart to develop, through a lifelong process, into a loving individual who experiences both day and night. And I have claimed that, in biblical terms, God knows each of us as a somebody, not a nobody. Only individual human beings, each with a name, have power to stand up every blessed doomsday to be, not counted, but recognized. That power freely to stand and freely to respond is the subject to which we now turn.

NOTES

1. J.A.T. Robinson, *The Body: A Study in Pauline Theology* (London: SCM Press, 1952), p. 14.

2. Rudolf Bultmann, *The Old and New Man* (Atlanta: John Knox Press, 1967), p. 20.

*Luther couldn't hack it either in the entirely monastic discipline. It's a good way to get a lot of work done in a short time but not a way to live a whole life.

3. Robinson, *The Body,* p. 14.

4. Ibid., p. 25. See the discussion of Paul's understanding of "flesh" and "spirit" in Eduard Schweizer, *The Holy Spirit* (Philadelphia: Fortress Press, 1980), pp. 80–84.

5. Bultmann, *Man,* p. 37.

6. St. Augustine, *Confessions* V, 20.

7. Laurens van der Post, *Jung and the Story of Our Time* (New York: Random House, 1977), p. 120.

8. James W. Heisig, "Jung and the Imago Dei: The Future of an Idea," *Journal of Religion* 56 (1976): 95.

9. van der Post, *Jung,* p. 60.

10. Heisig, "Jung and the Imago Dei," p. 104.

11. Ann Belford Ulanov, *The Feminine in Jungian Psychology and in Christian Theology* (Evanston, Ill.: Northwestern University Press, 1971), p. 71.

12. Ibid., p. 164.

13. June Singer, *Androgyny: Toward a New Theory of Sexuality* (New York: Doubleday & Co., 1977), p. 261.

14. Ibid., p. 213.

15. Johannes Pedersen, *Israel* (London: Oxford University Press, 1940), Vol. I–II, p. 256.

16. Acts 8:16, for example. See also Lars Hartman, "Baptism 'Into the Name of Jesus' and Early Christology," *Studia Theologica* 28 (1974): 21–48.

17. Phyllis Chesler, *Women and Madness* (New York: Avon Books, 1972), pp. 25–31.

18. Lyman Abbot, as quoted by Dorothy Bass Fraser, "The Feminine Mystique: 1890–1910," *Union Seminary Quarterly Review* 27 (1972): 235.

CHAPTER SIX

Free and Responsible

Well before the Emancipation Proclamation (1862) had been issued in these United States, the Congregational clergy of New England put forth a pastoral letter against a remarkable Christian who was speaking out against human slavery. The text of the letter was read aloud in pulpits from Bridgeport to Bangor. It evoked the authority of the New Testament to silence the proponent of freedom. The Bible, it said, teaches us that women should never speak out in public. Women who aspire to be elm trees instead of vines will topple into the dust.

Sarah Grimké, that outspoken abolitionist, had a different reading of the New Testament. She found no mention there, she said in her reply,[1] either of elm trees or clinging vines. Instead she found in scripture a commandment—given equally to everyone made in the image of God—to love our neighbors as ourselves. Thus in her judgment both women and men are charged to speak out in behalf of human freedom. Both men and women are equally responsible before God for the use of their own freedom to promote the freedom of others.

As we turn to look at freedom and responsibility, two more essential aspects of human personhood, we enter a confused landscape. Discussions of human freedom over the centuries have frequently bogged down because people were talking about two or

77

more different things. We will look at three major ideas of what freedom means. Philosophers and theologians have given them other labels, but I shall call them *crossroads freedom, checkbook freedom,* and *Christian freedom.* Each has as its corollary a different sense of responsibility.

(1) *Crossroads freedom* is that capacity we have to decide whether to turn left or right at a fork in the road. It is the power of choice each of us exercises whenever we drive a car, order a meal from a restaurant menu, or select clothes to put on in the morning. Whatever determinists tell us to the contrary, we all have the conviction that we could have chosen otherwise. Naively or not, we are sure that we could have taken another exit from the freeway, ordered lamb chops instead of fried chicken, or appeared shod in black shoes instead of brown.

Many of the early Christian Fathers considered this basic human liberty definitive of our reflection of the divine nature. Irenaeus, for example, said in the second century, "Man is free in will from the beginning, and free in will is God, to whose likeness he was made. . . ."[2] Similarly Basil of Caesarea said in the fourth century that the human soul was "set free of all compulsion and received from the Creator a life of free choice, because it was made to God's image."[3] His contemporaries shared the same understanding of the *imago dei.* We resemble God because we are free to choose what pleases us; we are not enslaved by any external compulsion. We are free, therefore, to choose to do right instead of wrong. Only if we have this freedom of will, these theologians believed, can we be found guilty for choosing to do evil. Our concrete freedom rests in our ability to refuse the evil and choose the good.

A distinguished cast of theologians has defended this very attractive view of human freedom, even while wrestling with the fact of experience that we refuse the good and choose the evil more often than not. Shortly after his conversion from the Manichean religion, St. Augustine, for example, wrote a treatise on free will dealing with the question of the origin of evil. At that point in his life, he thought it came from misuse of our freedom, and that through learning to love we can experience the true liberty of those "who cleave to the eternal law."[4]

Similarly, St. Anselm, "the father of scholasticism," insisted in a

78 ✻ *To believe such is to profoundly underestimate the power and pervasiveness of sin in ourselves and in our world. No choice is so simple as to involve alternatives of total good or evil. (See Rubin on making choices & McDonald on parable of wheat & tares*

treatise on "Freedom of Choice," written around A.D. 1080, that freedom is a constituent part of the *imago dei*. We have the ability, if not the motivation, to "keep uprightness" for its own sake.[5] And at the time of the Reformation, Erasmus made free will the target of his attack on Luther, on the grounds that without it human beings are mere puppets. "To what does the whole man avail," he asked, "if God so works in him as a potter with clay, and just as he could act on a pebble?"[6]

An equally distinguished list of theologians has denied that we have any such crossroads freedom. In his later years, Augustine, wearied by his fight against the pull-up-your-socks-and-fly-right moralism of the Pelagians, attributed less and less to human freedom. In a tract called "On Grace and Free Choice," written in A.D. 426, he said, "God brings about our willing without us."[7] Luther, in his bombastic reply to Erasmus, *On the Bondage of the Will*, decided that we must deny free will altogether and ascribe all good works to God alone. The great American theologian, Jonathan Edwards, also wrote a treatise rejecting all arguments in favor of free will and attributing all choice of the good to the irresistible action of God the Holy Spirit.

Anyone who reads these often arid debates in the history of theology quickly comes to the conclusion that our forefathers were treating a profound mystery of human experience as if it were a problem in logic. Why I choose to do evil when consciously I would prefer to do good cannot be reduced to the same terms as why I choose to turn left instead of right at the stoplight. The notion of crossroads freedom oversimplifies. It makes an intellectual puzzle out of a paradoxical religious experience. It leads our thinking into an either/or trap.

The question of "free will" all too often became an academic question about a purely formal idea of freedom. A second kind of freedom which must be distinguished is far from an academic matter. It concerns starving people, millions of starving people who have no energy to reflect on what the Bible means by claiming that we are made in the image of God. The Peruvian priest, Gustavo Gutierrez, has observed that where hunger is, God is not. Certainly where hunger is, freedom is not.

This second idea of freedom has usefully been labeled "circum-

79

stantial" freedom. To what extent do my living conditions permit me to exercise any human capacities worthy of the name of freedom? By using the label *checkbook freedom,* I intend to underline its minority status among the human race. Very few of us made in the image of God carry checkbooks or any other badge of human escape from bondage to necessity.

Many of the contemporary theologies of liberation, especially those born in Asia, Africa, and Latin America, concentrate on this basic human freedom, freedom to live. A large portion of the more than two billion men and women and children on those continents live on the razor's edge of survival. From one-third to one-half of them suffer from malnutrition and near-starvation. The life expectancy of the average person is twenty years less than that in the affluent world. Millions of them are illiterate.

Statistics, however, do not help people who enjoy three balanced meals a day to visualize the real situation of the people whom the Brazilian Paulo Freire describes as living corpses, shadows of human beings hopelessly battling against hunger and the myriad diseases of poverty.[8] In Brazil many people, it is alleged, sell themselves or members of their families into slavery in order to escape from hunger. To test that allegation, a newspaperman (it is reported) purchased a husband and wife for thirty dollars. When interviewed the male slave said, "I have seen many a good man starve; that is why I did not mind being sold."[9]

In such cultures the struggle for human freedom begins with the struggle for daily bread. The petition from the Lord's Prayer cannot be spiritualized. Jesus' bias on behalf of the poor, his mission to set at liberty those who are oppressed, is central to the Christian gospel. As he reflects on that gospel, Gustavo Gutierrez, author of *A Theology of Liberation,* thinks of freedom from oppression as freedom for developing one's own human potential. Not many of his fellow citizens have that chance.

The poor in Latin America are nonpersons, Gutierrez says. When he talks of "Faith as Freedom" he is calling for solidarity with these, the alienated—for a political faith instead of a faith lived in privacy and a love that will not leave its own backyard. Such public faith is concerned with doing justice, with changing social structures; but it is also intent on creating a new person, one "who is freer and freer of all kinds of servitudes that make it impossible for him to be the agent of his own destiny."[10]

The point is not to get the affluent to do good unto the poor, but to help the marginal members of society gain the power to write, as it were, their own checks. Along with Dom Helder Camara, Archbishop in Northeast Brazil, in the early sixties Paulo Freire founded a movement for basic education. Their goal was not only to teach people how to read but also to teach them to read about their basic human rights, and how to speak out for obtaining justice. Gutierrez also wants everyone to be free to speak out, to speak his or her own word. To this end, he calls on the church to speak out in denunciation of the oppressive social order, within the church as well as without.

Freedom from hunger and freedom for self-determination are closely linked to the global fight for basic human rights. At a World Council of Churches consultation on "Human Rights and Christian Responsibility" in Austria in October, 1974, David Jenkins argued that human rights are not absolutes, not things in themselves. His insights are helpful.

Much of the struggle for human rights, Jenkins thinks, must be interpreted as "*protests* about something wrong or dehumanizing and about experienced limitations on freedom." We need to think less of rights as possessions and more of removing obstacles to the relationships of love and enjoyment for which we were created. In fighting for the removal of those obstacles, he says, we must never forget what the human face represents. For "true humanity lies in the freedom and fulfillment of face-to-face relationships."[11]

This brings us back to the central theme of being human in the image of God. Freedom, along with other dimensions of our humanness, can best be understood in dynamic terms of relatedness. This means that it can best be understood in terms of our relationship to Jesus Christ. We must think about the third type of freedom, which is neither natural nor circumstantial but acquired. Freedom of this sort comes as a gift.

Before we leave checkbook freedom, however, an observation about responsibility is in order. To talk of freedom for our starving sisters and brothers can cause inordinate guilt feelings among those who have checking accounts. Those cast in the role of oppressor are usually not in that role through their own free choice. And, as a World Council of Churches statement on "Structures of Captivity and Lines of Liberation" noted, "Affluence is not liberation. Meaninglessness, loss of identity, despair and fear stalk the communities of the affluent in all countries."[12]

Alongside freedom of choice and freedom of circumstance— transcending crossroads and checkbooks—stands the paradox of *Christian freedom.* "For freedom Christ has set us free" is Paul's ringing cry to the Galatians (5:1). Yet that gift of freedom is given by one who took the form of a slave for our sakes, and who calls us to perfect freedom in his service.

Some critics think that the recent translation of much theology into the idiom of liberation has been overdone. Perhaps so. But it would be difficult to exaggerate the central role which the motif of freedom plays in the whole biblical record. From beginning to end God makes himself known as one who frees people from bondage. His people Israel know themselves as those who were delivered from slavery in Egypt. Although the noun freedom appears in the Torah only once, verbs of liberty and actions of liberation create and sustain the people of God. Therefore they sing: "We have heard with our ears, O God, our fathers have told us, what deeds thou didst perform in their days . . . them thou didst set free" (Ps. 44:1–2).

When the Christian church, thinking of itself as the New Israel, came to interpret the meaning of its experience of the life and death and resurrection of Jesus Christ according to Scripture, it was natural for it to recycle this inherited imagery. Two of its early theologians, St. Paul and the author of the Fourth Gospel, made the idea of freedom so important in their writings that one modern commentary on Paul's letter to the Romans was legitimately entitled, *Way of Freedom,*[13] and one on John's gospel *Liberation Theology.*[14] A third book published in the seventies, dealing with the whole range of New Testament writings, bore the equally appropriate title, *Jesus Means Freedom.*[15]

The theme of the World Council of Churches meeting in Nairobi, Kenya in 1975 was "Jesus as the one who frees and unites us." When Robert McAfee Brown addressed that Assembly, he raised the question, "Who is this Christ who frees . . . ?" He asked

82 *"Salvation" - to make broad - is probably far more descriptive and much more frequently used than our notion of freedom. "Salvation" has built into it the notion of gift and relatedness to God.*

the delegates to consider both the social and the individual consequences of encounter with Jesus the Liberator. In particular, he
asked those who found their hope in Jesus the Revolutionary to
hear also the Jesus "who reminds you that evil is embodied not
only in oppressive social structures but also in every human
heart. . . ."[16] Paul asks us to believe, as we shall see shortly, that
Jesus delivers us from the tyranny of that heart. But first, what of
Jesus' own personal experience of freedom?

Jesus did not talk much about freedom. Indeed, the noun is
never on his lips in the synoptic gospels, and the adjective "free"
only once (Matt. 17:26). But both his actions and his words showed
what personal freedom looks like. Remembering once again the
Pauline tradition that calls Christ *the* image of God, we can see why
it is possible to claim that *imago dei* includes the idea of human
freedom.

The Jesus whom we meet through the synoptic gospels is a person remarkably free from bondage to his own culture—to the social, political, and religious conventions of his own time and place.
We have already noted the great variety of people with whom he
is said to have talked. Devout Jews of his day did not talk with
women in public. They did not go out of their way to help either
those who collaborated with the Romans or the officers of that
occupying army. And they certainly did not harvest crops on the
Sabbath or disrupt business in the temple.

An unconventional person is not necessarily a free one, however.
Jesus showed his personal freedom, in addition, by his actions in
freeing others. People who had suffered crippling physical disa-
bilities for years were enabled to stand straight again and walk
again, and see and hear and speak. People long haunted by de-
mons were released to be themselves.

The authority with which Jesus spoke was the authority of a
liberated human being. That quality of authority which the gospel
writers attribute to him twenty-nine times was not the quality of
officiousness which we sometimes confuse with authority, nor of
a martinet determined to get his own way. Rather it was an authority exercised by word of freedom.

Above all, Jesus spoke and acted as one who is freed from the
delusion of his own autonomy. His transcendent freedom appears

83

to have been the fruit of his radical faith in God, of his complete dependence on his heavenly Father, of his freely offered obedience. Jesus, as the gospels picture him, is a man of prayer. Jürgen Moltmann thinks that freedom starts here. "How does freedom thus begin? It begins with prayer, with the permission to be different, and with the way into the joy of God. Where does it end? It ends in the new creation of all things and relationships."[17]

Jesus himself, as freedom incarnate, then, may have been free because he knew he was loved. Peter C. Hodgson, in his stimulating theology of bondage and freedom, has analyzed Jesus' own freedom and drawn from that analysis a Christian "symbolics" of freedom. The man Jesus of Nazareth exhibited radical freedom in his openness to God, in his existence for others, and in his personal identity—his own sense of selfhood. To amplify the last of these, selfhood, Hodgson chooses the Johannine category of "life." Human life, he says, connotes "an integrated self-conscious subjectivity based upon a personal body, issuing in joy, celebration, play."[18] That quality of life might equally well be designated "liveliness." It can be contrasted with the state of people in bondage to repressions, those who enclose the self in constricting defense systems and lose their liveliness. The opposite of the liveliness of Jesus in this sense is apathy.

What Jesus accomplished in terms of a new understanding of human freedom, Hodgson suggests, was a reversal of the old (and not so old) humanistic structure of the idea of freedom. Instead of beginning with the idea that he was a law unto himself, he began with obedience to God. The end product was free personal identity and authority, a life qualified by faith and love, and opened to the kingdom of freedom.

In contrast to Jesus' reticence in speaking of freedom, St. Paul used it as a key category in his correspondence with Christians in Galatia, Corinth, and Rome. To avoid over-systematizing Paul's thought, we will look at what he says to the Christians in each of these places about their new liberties.

The people to whom Paul wrote in Galatia, in what is now Turkey, were evidently finding it difficult to live with their new-found freedom. They were falling back again to "a yoke of slavery." It is not clear in detail what that yoke was which the Galatians found

*Spontaneity means "free to function"; *uberotto*

more attractive than the good news which Paul had preached to them, but it certainly had to do with careful attention to religious observances—with being circumcised, with works of the law, with observing "days, and months, and seasons" (Gal. 4:10).

In his "Cotton Patch" version of this letter, Clarence Jordan transposes the desire for religious security that was bewitching the Galatians into the desire to protect "the Southern way of life," keeping the taboos, upholding the old traditions. He paraphrases Gal. 4:31–5:2:

> . . . we are not children of a *slave* system, but of a free society. It was for this freedom that Christ emancipated us. So stand your ground, and don't let anybody saddle you with that slave system again. Look here, I Paul himself, am telling you that if you accept segregation, Christ isn't worth a cent to you.[19]

Whether one thinks of circumcision or segregation, the problem lies in relying on the system. We cannot do anything as part of the system (or on our own) to achieve a right relationship with God. Paul says, of course, that we are free from the curse of legalisms and of all efforts at self-justification because of Christ's death on the cross. Jesus' self-giving has given us freedom for faith in him and for new relationships with one another. The extent to which he frees us from false securities by which we try to make our lives secure is summed up in the sentence:

> There is neither Jew nor Greek, there is neither slave nor free, there is neither male nor female; for you are all one in Christ Jesus.
> (Gal. 3:28)

The new gift of freedom is not to be confused with permission to do anything you want, however. As a corollary of being set free from old definitions of who's who, we are enabled to become servants of one another through love. Before the end of his letter, Paul amplifies the servant metaphor. Now we are able to bear one another's burdens, to shoulder each other's loads.

The letter to the Galatians has been called "the Magna Charta of spiritual emancipation," but Paul himself never reached the logical conclusion that something is wrong with the institution of human slavery. His conviction that the time of the world had grown very short undoubtedly helps account for that failure, as the context of his admonition that slaves should not mind being slaves indicates (1 Corinthians 7). But even if we can exonerate him personally, we should not overlook the fact that Mississippi slave owners used the example of this apostle of freedom to indoctrinate their slaves. One catechism used for slaves in 1857 reads:

> Q. Should servants ever run away?
> A. No. If they do, they sin against God and man.
> Q. How do you know this?
> A. The Bible tells us that the apostle Paul found a servant who had run away from his master, and he sent him home.
> Q. Why did not Paul conceal him, that he might be free?
> A. Because he would not make religion a cloak for injustice.[20]

Today we read Paul's letter to Philemon in a different light; but whatever his reasons for not challenging the social institution of slavery, he was deeply convinced that true freedom is a gift given to us when we become slaves to Christ and to each other. Twice in his "first" letter to his friends in Corinth he directly affirms that paradox. "For he who was called in the Lord as a slave is a freedman of the Lord. Likewise he who was free when called is a slave of Christ" (1 Cor. 7:22). The same contrast applies to his own ministry. "For though I am free from all men, I have made myself a slave to all, that I might win the more" (9:19).

Paul's theology of the new freedom in Christ is worked out more thoroughly in his letter to the Romans. It is possible that the house churches in that imperial capital were experiencing tensions among themselves—between Jewish-Christian congregations bent on maintaining their traditions and others who were rejoicing in freedom from the past. If so, that would have made his message about "the way of freedom" ring louder in the ears of those who heard themselves addressed as "called to belong to Jesus Christ." Those who put their trust in Christ, Paul argues, are freed from the enslaving powers of Wrath, Sin, Law, and Death. They are set free to walk in newness of life, the life which Jesus makes available through his death and resurrection. To walk in that life is to walk in love, an event of freedom. Indeed Paul contends that this "glorious liberty of the children of God" will ultimately extend to the whole of creation (Rom. 8:21). Liberation appears as the over-arching work of God.

86 *Paul follows Jesus role model of the servant

If for Paul freedom signifies not just a natural capacity of the self but a relationship, the same is true for the author of the Gospel of John, but with his own distinctive twist. The language of freedom is explicit in only one section of the gospel, John 8:31–36, as part of Jesus' discourses at the time of the Feast of Tabernacles, a feast associated both with the triumphant Day of the Lord and with the seasonal rains which replenish the earth. Jesus tells his hearers that if they continue in his word they are truly his disciples. "And you will know the truth, and the truth will make you free" (8:32).

Those who inscribe these words, ripped from their context, on the facades of libraries open them to misunderstanding as great as that shown by the Jews who answered Jesus. We are the descendants of Abraham, they boasted, and have never been anyone's slaves. Jesus clarifies the matter. The slaves in question are slaves of sin. In contrast to such slaves, the Son is free. When he sets people free they are free indeed. Thus, in terms of the Fourth Gospel, knowing the truth, experiencing freedom, means knowing Jesus.

So far in this chapter we have discussed three types of human freedom. The first type, *crossroads freedom,* was simply that freedom of choice to turn left or right, to do right or wrong. In our common experience we think we have this kind of free choice, whatever the behaviorists think, and so we feel responsible for doing what we know we ought to do and guilty when we don't. On this level we live according to the law. The second type, *checkbook freedom,* was that freedom of circumstance which permits a relatively small percentage of the human race to enjoy the fruits of the earth, while the majority remains enslaved by poverty. Once again a burden of guilt is the consequence of reflection on this second kind of freedom.

The third type, *Christian freedom,* is the gift of new relationship with God, with each other, and with ourselves. Both St. Paul and St. John say it is a gift from Jesus Christ. It frees us from our slavery to the old system and its old guilt trips. Before concluding this discussion, however, we must be more explicit about the kind of responsibility which is the corollary of this *Christian freedom.* For no one given this gift is free to go about muttering pious prayers and forgetting the rest of the human race. No adequate Christian understanding of free persons can glibly offer the slogan "Jesus means Freedom" as sufficient answer to the complex issues of social bondage.

Jesus of Nazareth is not only the paradigm of the free human being. He is also the paradigm of the responsible human being. Use of the word "responsible" to mean accountable is relatively new in the language, as H. Richard Niebuhr pointed out in his reflections on *The Responsible Self*.[21] In its root sense the word means responsiveness. We are creatures who respond, who answer to questions addressed to us, who act and react to actions upon us. Jesus epitomizes human responsiveness in his continuing dialogue with God and in his ready replies to human pleas for help.

But further, through his life, death, and resurrection, and through the gift of his Spirit, he empowers a new response, a new responsiveness in those who are learning to turn around and trust him. Niebuhr speaks of redemption as "the liberty to interpret in trust all that happens."[22] Paul speaks of the same liberty when he says, "Now the Lord is the Spirit, and where the Spirit of the Lord is, there is freedom" (2 Cor. 3:17).

From this perspective, responsibility becomes a thankful response for a Pentecostal present (as well as for those of Christmas and Easter). We are invited to think of responsibility as a eucharistic "therefore." It was no accident that Paul, having described how we are set free from alien slavemasters, as he knew himself to be, launched into a great ethical peroration in his letter to the Romans: "I appeal to you therefore . . ." The appeal? To owe no one anything, except to love one another.

One final thing must be said about the responsible selfhood which is responsive to the freedom that is gift. We can so respond only because we know ourselves to be forgiven over and over again. The freedom from the tyranny of sin about which Paul and John write reinforces the already-but-not-yet quality of our lives at the intersection of two aeons. And so we pray daily, "Forgive us our sins."

Forgiveness, as Evelyn Underhill once remarked, is not the easy passage of a sponge over a slate. It is, rather, a painful process. Forgiveness means the reordering of our disordered love. For we

88

human beings, especially those with *checkbook freedom,* have abused the sacred gift of freedom. And because of us things are worse than they might be.

NOTES

1. Sarah Grimké, *Letters on the Equality of the Sexes* (New York: Burt Franklin, 1970; first published, 1838), pp. 14–21.

2. Irenaeus, *Adversus haereses* IV, 60, 2 as cited by Walter J. Burghardt, S.J., *The Image of God in Man According to Cyril of Alexandria* (Woodstock, Md.: Woodstock College Press, 1957), p. 40.

3. Basil of Caesarea, *Quod Deus non est auctor malorum* 6, as cited ibid., p. 43.

4. John H. S. Burleigh, ed., *Augustine: Earlier Writings* (Philadelphia: Westminster Press, 1953), p. 132.

5. St. Anselm, in Jasper Hopkins and Herbert Richardson, eds., *Truth, Freedom and Evil: Three Philosophical Dialogues* (New York: Harper & Row, Torchbooks, 1967), p. 140.

6. Erasmus, in E. Gordon Rupp, ed., *Luther and Erasmus on Free Will* (Philadelphia: Westminster Press, 1969), p. 96.

7. This statement is later qualified in his *Retractions.*

8. Paulo Freire, *Pedagogy of the Oppressed* (New York: Seabury Press, 1973), p. 172.

9. John Gerassi, *The Great Fear in Latin America* (New York: Collier Macmillan, 1966).

10. Gustavo Gutierrez, "Faith as Freedom," *Horizons* 2 (1975): 34. See also *A Theology of Liberation: History, Politics, and Salvation* (Maryknoll, N.Y.: Orbis Books, 1973).

11. David Jenkins, *The Ecumenical Review* 27 (1975): 102.

12. "Structures of Captivity and Lines of Liberation," *The Ecumenical Review* 27 (1975): 44.

13. Christopher Bryan, *Way of Freedom: An Introduction to the Epistle to the Romans* (New York: Seabury Press, 1972).

14. Frederick Herzog, *Liberation Theology: Liberation in the Light of the Fourth Gospel* (New York: Seabury Press, 1972).

15. Ernst Käsemann, *Jesus Means Freedom* (Philadelphia: Fortress Press, 1970).

16. Robert McAfee Brown, "Who is This Jesus Christ who Frees and Unites? *The Witness* 61 (1976): 7.

17. Jürgen Moltmann, *The Gospel of Liberation* (Waco, Texas: Word, 1973), p. 24.

18. Peter C. Hodgson, *New Birth of Freedom: A Theology of Bondage and Liberation* (Philadelphia: Fortress Press, 1976), p. 227.

19. Clarence Jordan, *The Cotton Patch Version of Paul's Epistles* (New York: Association Press, 1968).

20. Gilbert Osofsky, ed., *Puttin' on Ole Massa* (New York: Harper & Row, 1969), p. 33.

21. H. Richard Niebuhr, *The Responsible Self* (New York: Harper & Row, 1963), p. 56.

22. Ibid., p. 142.

CHAPTER SEVEN

Imaginative Creatures

Because we have been given the gift of freedom we human beings are able to see that things might be other than they are. We have the capacity to emerge from the cocoon of our own here and now, to project ourselves into the past and into the future. We are enabled to see through eyes other than our own. Through the exercise of our God-given imagination, we can get outside of our own skins and think what it might be like to be someone else. And so we are enabled to create and to love.

One of the most distinctive qualities of Homo sapiens, theologians have long told us, is rationality. Indeed "the Fathers" of theology almost universally located "the image of God" in the mind or *nous*. But when they did so they were operating with a far richer concept of mind than most of us operate with today. When Augustine of Hippo, for example, found a trinitarian image of God in his mind, he reflected on self-knowledge in terms of memory, understanding, and will. In another triad of experience with which he played, love is one of the terms. His essay on such trinities ends in prayer. It is no mere head trip.

From at least the seventeenth century until the very recent past, however, the idea of what it means to be a rational animal shrank drastically. To change the metaphor, mind suffered a compound fracture. Not one but three splits occurred. Thinking was isolated

91

from feelings, "objectivity" from "subjectivity," reason from imagination. As a result science was divorced from poetry. And sons were separated from daughters.

Intellectual history since the end of World War II shows a clear trend back toward a more unified notion of what it means to be human. The beginnings of the healing process are visible even earlier. Nineteenth-century Romanticists like the English poet William Blake and the German poet Novalis, like Samuel Coleridge in England and Horace Bushnell in America, worked to restore the imagination. When bombs rained on Cologne and London, however, many more men and women came to see the urgency of putting their viscera back together with their heads.

In those war years one theologian shuddered deeply at the manifest results of three centuries of bias in favor of analysis, yet she was optimistic enough to assert that "there are signs everywhere that the human mind is once more beginning to move towards a synthesis of experience."[1] While she was looking forward to the day when artists and scientists could once more talk to each other, C. S. Lewis was looking for the reconciliation of imagination and reason within himself. Using the figures of Demeter and Athene to personify the two, Lewis wrote:

> Oh who will reconcile in me both maid and mother,
> Who will make in me a concord of the depth and height?
> Who make imagination's dim exploring touch
> Ever report the same as intellectual sight?[2]

If a generation ago most people equated rationality largely with powers of analysis and logic, and called them masculine traits, we are increasingly aware today that all creative thought depends on leaps of imagination as well as on problem-solving techniques. Scientists cannot get along without inspiration and "subjectivity" any more than poets can get along without the laboratory of experience and the "objectivity" of honed metaphor. Because we are again able to celebrate the left hand along with the right, perhaps both our daughters and our sons will share in the new age of the Spirit which reverses the confusion of Babel.

Now I want to look more closely at human beings as creative and imaginative beings—beings in the process of discovering who we are. I propose that our capacity for *memory, laughter,* and *dreams*

92

contributes to that discovery. It is true that we can rightly talk about a corporate memory, about shared laughter and common dreams; but these are nevertheless matters of great individuality. My memories are different from yours. Your sense of humor is different from mine. The dreams of each of us are introduced by our own theme song. Here again we wear our own name tags. Here again we live in the first person singular.

St. Augustine himself, that great African whom the church celebrates as the Doctor of Grace, celebrated *memory*. He called it "the belly of the mind."[3] A modern interpreter therefore likens Augustine's concept of memory to our contemporary myths of the "unconscious" and the "subconscious."[4] Although Augustine lacked some of our latter-day tools of analysis and research, he remains one of history's most perceptive psychologists.

When he explored his own memory, Augustine found "innumerable images" stored in its "spacious palaces." He compared his memory to "a great harbour" with "numberless secret and inexpressible windings," or again to a treasure house "wonderfully furnished with innumerable stores." Taking inventory of those stores, Augustine finds that they include images originally imbibed through the senses. Heaven, earth, and sea are present with him there. Thanks to memory he can see again, smell again, and hear again. "And though my tongue be still, and my throat mute, so can I sing as much as I will."[5] His memory also includes feelings such as joy and sorrow. He marvels that he can remember sorrow without pain and even with joy.

Convinced that memory is the deepest part of the human self or soul, Augustine believed that it was his true self: "Great is the power of memory, a fearful thing, O my God, a deep and boundless manifoldness; and this thing is the mind, and this am I myself."[6] He also believed that in his memory he could meet and delight in God.

In the *Confessions* Augustine insists that he is not recollecting a God whom he knew in some previous existence. But ever since he learned to know God, he says, he has not forgotten him. "Since then I learned Thee, Thou residest in my memory; and there do I find Thee, when I call Thee to remembrance, and delight in Thee."[7]

When Augustine contemplates God's image in himself, as in his essay *On the Trinity*, he again contemplates the human mind. It is "an image—inadequate indeed, but still truly an image" of the Triune God.[8] As he develops his notion of memory, understanding, and will, with full recognition of the limitations of his own analogy, it is memory which is analagous to God the Father. From the store-chamber of memory, when we speak what we know, a true word is begotten. Such true words are "locutions of the heart." The mind which this profound student of himself investigated proved on inspection to be manifold and mysterious.

The workings of the memory are still a mystery to modern scientists, psychologists, and philosophers. The noted neurophysiologist, Sir John Eccles, made memory the subject of one of his 1977–78 Gifford Lectures at Edinburgh on the topic *The Human Mystery*. He reported, "It is not yet possible to investigate in any meaningful manner the actual neural events that are of crucial importance in the laying down of a memory."[9] In his book *On Knowing: Essays for the Left Hand*,[10] Jerome Bruner, the former Harvard psychologist now at Oxford, reported on some modern efforts to discover more about it. In Bruner's terms the right hand is the doer; the left hand, the dreamer.

In one of the experiments Bruner describes, twelve-year-olds were asked to remember thirty pairs of words, such as chair-forest or sidewalk-square. Half of the subjects were simply told to memorize them because they should be prepared to repeat them later. The other half were invited to think up some special way to remember them. The first group scored less than fifty percent recall. The second group, those who had devised their own way of remembering, scored up to ninety-five percent.

The children in this second group used three different kinds of mnemonic devices. Some remembered by what Bruner calls "generic mediation." They used the clue, for example, that chairs and forests are both made of wood. Others made up stories. A little girl, lost in the forest, sat down on a chair. Or finally, some came up with a part-whole scheme, remembering the idea that chairs are one of the things made out of the trees of a forest.

These three methods of remembering were equally useful. What mattered, as Bruner reports it, was that the child had contributed his or her own organizational principle to the cognitive process. Bruner believes that memory and discovery are interdependent. New insights are inseparable from old facts. Discovery, he says, "favors the well-prepared mind."

Reflecting on the nature of science, Michael Polanyi came to remarkably similar conclusions about the relationships between memory and that mysterious leap into new knowledge which we call discovery. He, too, was interested in mnemonic devices. They belong, he said, among "the anticipatory powers which guide discovery."[11]

Polanyi relates what he calls "ransacking" our memories to heuristics, the art of discovery. Discovery is at least fifty percent dependent on relating the unknown to the known. Unless you are acquainted with the solution of past problems, you are not in a position to solve current ones.

In language which shows that he has been in conversation with Augustine on the subject of memory, Polanyi discusses looking for a lost fountain pen. It is somewhere in my apartment. I am sure of that. But I can't find it. I could, of course, conduct a systematic search of my apartment from stem to stern; but I can find my pen much more quickly, Polanyi argues, by searching in my head. My search illustrates the "simplest heuristic effort." Discovering where it is will entail "a leap beyond logic." That is the nature of a heuristic act.

The success of my mental search depends, it appears to Polanyi, on two factors. First, I must remember what my pen looks like. I cannot find it unless I know what I am looking for. And secondly, "the more theorems I can remember" about where it might be, the more likely I am to find it.

Polanyi's analysis of this process of discovery then moves to the name one has forgotten. Who was that person I encountered on the bus? Her name is "on the tip of my tongue." "It will come to me in a moment." The process is the same, he says, in the case of rediscovering a mislaid pen, remembering a forgotten name, or solving an unfamiliar problem. First, we believe that there is an answer, a solution. (Polanyi understands belief as the source of all knowledge.) Second, we focus our attention on the problem, translating it into symbolic terms, the better to juggle it. Thirdly, we may just have to wait. There is, Polanyi thinks, a period of incubation, a period of repose, during which our "intellectual strivings" make effective progress without our conscious effort. The fourth and final stage is "Eureka! I have it!"

Both Bruner and Polanyi offer splendid examples of our need to broaden once again our understanding of thinking and knowing. But they are both handicapped in their thinking by the idea that problem-solving is the key demand on those rational powers. Indeed, Bruner's discussion of information storage and retrieval seems to be informed throughout by an underlying model of man-the-machine. He makes one want to insist that we must use human metaphors in thinking about who we are, lest we become trapped in the presupposition that we are preprogrammed robots.

Life, as Dorothy L. Sayers rightly notes in her discussion of the creating creature, is not primarily a problem to be solved. She thinks that the words "problem" and "solution" belong only to the analytic approach to phenomena, not to the creative. Careless use of the problem solving model can, she believes, keep us from asking the right question.

People read detective fiction, this creator of the eminent Lord Peter Wimsey series speculates, in order that they can be softly persuaded that "love and hatred, poverty and unemployment, finance and international politics, are problems capable of being dealt with and solved in the same manner as Death in the Library."[12] She draws four contrasts between the detective story and the human situation to show that that is not the case. The human situation calls for more creative thinking.

The detective problem is always solvable. It is constructed for that purpose. The question of creating a life is far different, because there is no solution to death. Second, when the detective story is solved there are no loose ends hanging out, no uncertainties left. Our desire to tidy up the human situation in a comparable manner leads to distorted expectations. For example, Sayers says, we expect doctors to know what is wrong with us and solve the problem. Instead, she thinks, we should realize that the physician is performing an adventurous and creative act which needs the creative cooperation of the patient.

In the third place, the author of the detective story must solve the story-problem in the terms in which it is set. If we are to change our life situations, we must frequently alter the terms as they present themselves. One of her examples of this contrast is unemployment. What we need, she thinks, is a totally new set of questions about work and money. Instead of trying to solve a problem, we need to create a new way of life. And finally, when the detective story is solved, that's the end of it. We can close the book. Not so with such matters as world peace. No talks in Geneva or Jerusalem can end the matter. Peace is "a work to be made," an unending creative work. Sayers's cautionary words about overuse of problem-solving in our thinking, however, are set forth in the form of a sharp rational analysis of the phenomenon. It is time that we laughed at ourselves.

If memory is a means whereby we exercise our imaginations and thereby discover that things might be other than they are, *laughter* is another. And it is a distinctively human gift. All organisms have some type of memory, it is said; but only human beings can manage the coordinated contraction of some fifteen facial muscles, accompanied by an altered state of breathing, which we call laughter. Arthur Koestler dubs laughter a luxury reflex.[13] *Homo ridens,* the laughing animal, could only emerge when the race had achieved enough relative security to allow for other uses of adrenalin. But with the emergence of a sense of humor came the capacity for self-criticism. We are able to laugh at ourselves.

Frederick Buechner, in his *Alphabet of Grace,* remembers a sermon he heard when he was twenty-seven. A famous New York preacher was talking about the coronation of Queen Elizabeth II and about the coronation of Jesus in the heart of the believer. Jesus, the preacher said, "is crowned among confession and tears and great laughter." At the phrase *great laughter,* Buechner recalls, "for reasons I have never satisfactorily understood, the great wall of China crumbled and Atlantis rose up out of the sea. . . ."[14]

Falling down and getting up again is at the heart of genuine laughter. The comic spirit, which appears to be built into the human mind, reminds us that no matter how many times we are knocked down we can pick ourselves up again. Comedy, it has been well said, adds resurrection to birth, struggle, and death.[15]

The Bible does not have very much use for laughter as such,

97

and for a very good reason. It recognizes the negative side of laughter, the malice and scorn and disbelief which can lie just beneath its surface. Sarah at the door of her tent eavesdropping on the conversation between Abraham and Yahweh is a classic example of this distrust of laughter. The postmenopausal woman laughed at the promise of a son. When she bore him, she said, "God has made laughter for me; everyone who hears will laugh over me" (Gen. 21:6). Being laughed at or over is clearly not a welcome experience.

In the New Testament the verb "to laugh" is used only in one story, one of disbelief. People laughed *at* Jesus when he told them that the little girl he was about to heal was not dead but sleeping (Mark 5:40 and par.). Yet he took her by the hand and raised her up. The noun "laughter" occurs just once in the whole New Testament corpus, and that in an entirely negative context. The author of James charges, "Let your laughter be turned to mourning and your joy to dejection. Humble yourselves . . ."(4:9–10).

Laughter, it appears, is another ambiguous human trait, neither all good nor all bad. But along with the biblical use of the words so translated must be set the cognate words for mirth and joy and gladness. Along with laughter, these bright emotions fill out the spectrum of that rainbow arching between death and life.

The biological basis of laughter is clear. It can, in fact, be called an instinct, however imprecise the use of that term. It can be described in relation to muscular contortions, changed breathing rates, and the use of adrenalin. Consider, however, the phenomenon of tickling. Is it only a sensory stimulus which causes a child to laugh when someone rubs fingertips over the soles of the feet? Careful studies on tickling suggest three reasons for answering no. We do not laugh when we tickle ourselves. Babies do not laugh as hard when the tickler is not someone they know and trust. The greatest laughter is evoked when the mock-aggressor is the one person most trusted, the mother. Of key importance in the fine art of tickling is an element of surprise.

Consider next the success with which Lucy annually makes Charlie Brown fall flat on his back: she holds the football for him to kick, and then withdraws it at the last moment as he swings his foot—up, up into the air. Charles M. Schultz is able to make many of us laugh year after year by the element of surprise which his creative imagination is able to add to this old routine. It is a now-classic variation on the theme of slipping on the banana peel, and as such the situation further illustrates the potentially cruel side of laughter. We enjoy seeing the mighty brought low—the school teacher's chair breaking beneath her, the string snapping on the concert violin.

But why should we laugh or even smile when Charlie Brown, the epitome of the underdog, falls yet once more on his back in the mud? I am not interested at this point in making lofty distinctions between what is funny and what is comic, as some of the literature does. I suggest that we laugh at Charlie Brown because we identify with him as much if not more than with Lucy, the trickster. We see ourselves being tricked and we are able to laugh because we know that Charlie Brown is going to get up out of the mud, and not let Lucy fool him in that particular way—until next year.

When Polanyi and Bruner talked about memory as an aid for discovery, they used problem-solving language which came close to promoting that activity to the chief function of the imagination. Wolfhart Pannenberg does much the same thing in a chapter translated under the title "Mastery of Existence Through Imagination."[16] If Dorothy L. Sayers and Charles M. Schultz are right, and I think they are, the attempt to master existence in the sense of getting the upper hand over ourselves and the world around us is a wrongheaded, or at best one-sided, use of our imaginative powers.

Consider, as a final illustration of the gift of humor, God and mud. One standard theory about the root of the comic, of course, is that it grows out of incongruity. There is an incontestable incongruity in pairing the exalted and the trivial, God and mud. And yet the link may best illustrate what William F. Lynch so well called "the courage of the comic." Lynch argues that the function of comedy "is to be a perpetual and funny, if disconcerting, reminder that it is the limited concrete which is the path to insight and salvation."[17]

When we excluded imagination from reason, banished the Feast of Fools from our liturgies, and enthroned Descartes as the arbiter of who we are, we lost touch with our full selves and our comic spirit. Both are rediscoverable, to use a phrase from Yeats, only in "all complexities of mire and blood." For three centuries, that is, we have suffered from the illusion that we are most fully human, most supremely rational animals, at higher and higher levels of abstraction.

When we come back to earth, back to the comic, back to the muddy concrete which is the source of "all the mighty energies of the imagination's bloodstream"[18] we come again to Jesus. We come to that upset of the established order which made the morning stars sing together and all the sons and daughters of God shout for joy. In "The Meditation of Simeon" W. H. Auden put these words into the mouth of Simeon:

> Because in Him the Word is united to the Flesh without loss of perfection, Reason is redeemed from incestuous fixation on her own Logic . . . in Him abstraction finds a passionate For-The-Sake-Of. . .[19]

It might be a jolt to pious sensibilities to call the *Magnificat* funny, but it is surely comic. I find that it has the same humorous surprise as Mr. Pompous brought low by the banana peel or Charlie Brown brought low because Lucy jerks the football out of the way when his punt is in full swing. Mary, rejoicing in God her Savior, shares "the courage of the comic." She can see that God "has scattered the proud in the imagination of their hearts, he has put down the mighty from their thrones, and exalted those of low degree" (Luke 2:51–52).

Nowhere does the New Testament record the fact that Jesus laughed, but he clearly calls upon us to laugh at ourselves. Lynch says that there is an anamnesis, a remembering, proper to the comic. A good example of that anamnesis is remembering the words of Jesus that this generation is like children who aren't happy playing either wedding games or funeral games. When John came, refusing to eat or drink, people said he had a demon. When the Son of man came eating and drinking, they called him a glutton and a drunkard (Matt. 11:16–18). Are we not being called to affirm a disorder which is "more muddy, more actual, more free"[20] than our anticipated order of how God ought to deal with us?

Dreaming, a third activity of our imagination, allows us to see

100

things differently; yet dreaming, like laughter, can be a negative as well as a positive experience. The child who wakens screaming from a nightmare is unlikely to agree with the modern theory that a dream life is essential to psychic health. She is more likely to agree with Job:

> When I say, "My bed will comfort me,
>   my couch will ease my complaint,"
> then thou dost scare me with dreams
>   and terrify me with visions.
>
> (Job 7:13–14)

Dreams and dreamers have an extraordinary prominence in the Bible. Joseph and Daniel are the Freud and Jung of the ancient world, establishing their reputations and royal incomes as interpreters of dreams. Two aspects of the biblical understanding, however, seem to illuminate our contemporary perception of what it means to include dreaming in our definition of human being. The first is the dream in the literal sense of images occurring during sleep. The second is the dream in the metaphoric sense of the waking vision.

Three classic dreams in the first category invite our attention. There is Jacob, camped out en route from Beersheba to Haran to find himself a wife (Gen. 28:10ff.). Since he is sleeping with his head on a rock, it is perhaps surprising that he did not have a nightmare. Instead he had a spiritual experience, a dream in which God spoke to him assuring him that he would be accompanied and guided by the divine presence.

The cherished symbolism of the ladder has to go, modern commentators tell us. The imagery is rather that of the wide stairway up to the top of a Babylonian ziggurat, wide enough for angels to ascend and descend without bumping each other off. Such an explanation seems to ignore the fact that the logic of dreams is not that of the waking state. But that quibble does not negate the main point. When Jacob awoke, he said, "Surely the Lord is in this place; and I did not know it" (Gen. 28:16). The episode suggests that we can discover reality at the level of our unconscious life perhaps more readily than when we are under the domination of our conscious expectations of a commonplace world.

Two other dreams through which God is said to have made

himself and his protective presence known are recorded in the Gospel according to Matthew, a gospel which shows more interest in dreams than the other New Testament writings. As you recall, it is through an angel of the Lord appearing in a dream that Joseph is persuaded to take the pregnant Mary as his wife (Matt. 1:20). And it is through a subsequent dream that he is warned to flee to Egypt until Herod dies, so that the child Jesus will be safe. One cannot help wondering, historically, how much the tradition of Joseph the dreamer in Genesis has influenced the Matthean picture of Joseph, the father of Jesus, as a dreamer, too; but that does not affect the theological point. As in the Old Testament, so in the New; people believed that God reveals himself to human beings through the dreams that happen while they are asleep. Dreams were already seen to be windows into reality deeper than our morning eyes can see.

Freud once wrote that the concept "No" does not seem to exist in the dream. Some dim recognition of that falsification of reality may lie behind the strand of biblical thought which links dreamers with false prophets. Deuteronomy offers a good example when it condemns to death any prophet or "dreamer of dreams" who tells people to go after false gods (Deut. 13:5). Jeremiah has a similar evaluation of prophetic dreaming: "Let the prophet who has a dream tell the dream, but let him who has my word speak my word faithfully. What has straw in common with wheat? says the Lord" (Jer. 23:28). Indeed, Jeremiah links prophets and dreamers with soothsayers, diviners, and sorcerers (27:9).

Nevertheless, there is a positive scriptural tradition linking dreamers with true prophets, with those who hear the Word of the Lord and speak it. It is out of that tradition that the prophet Joel spoke of the last days when God will pour out his Spirit on all flesh. It is out of that tradition that Luke interprets the experience of Pentecost as the fulfillment of that promise:

> I will pour out my Spirit upon all flesh,
> and your sons and your daughters shall prophesy,
> and your young men shall see visions,
> and your old men shall dream dreams.
>
> (Acts 2:17)

And it is out of that tradition also that Martin Luther King, Jr. stood up in Washington, D.C. in 1963 and altered history with the words, "I have a dream. . . ."

We allow the human imagination to atrophy at great peril, as I have suggested here. Abstraction, daylight logic, and their formulas led to Dachau and to Hiroshima. Imagination in full play—remembering, laughing, and dreaming—can lead to a selfhood which knits together past and future, mud and God, night and day. Only such a selfhood can sing with the Psalmist:

> When the Lord restored the fortunes of Zion,
>   we were like those who dream.
> Then our mouth was filled with laughter,
>   and our tongue with shouts of joy.

(Ps. 126:1–2)

NOTES

1. Dorothy L. Sayers, *Christian Letters to a Post-Christian World* (Grand Rapids, Mich.: Wm. B. Eerdmans Publishing Co., 1969), p. 106.

2. C. S. Lewis, *Poems* (New York: Harcourt, Brace, Jovanovich, 1964), as quoted by Kathryn Lindskoog, "Getting It Together: C. S. Lewis and the Two Hemispheres of Knowing," *Journal of Psychology and Theology* 3 (1975): 291.

3. St. Augustine, *The Confessions* X, 20.

4. John Burnaby in his introduction to *Augustine: Later Works* (Philadelphia: Westminster Press, 1955), p. 35.

5. St. Augustine, *The Confessions* X (VIII), 13.

6. Ibid., (XVII) 26.

7. Ibid., (XXIV) 35.

8. Burnaby, *Augustine*, p. 89.

9. Sir John Eccles, *The Human Mystery* (New York: Springer, 1979), p. 189.

10. Jerome Bruner, *On Knowing: Essays for the Left Hand* (New York: Atheneum, 1965).

11. Michael Polanyi, *Personal Knowledge: Towards a Post-Critical Philosophy* (New York: Harper & Row, 1964), p. 124.

12. Sayers, *Christian Letters*, p. 112.

13. Arthur Koestler, *The Act of Creation* (New York: Dell Publishing Co., 1964), p. 31.

14. Frederick Buechner, *Alphabet of Grace* (New York: Seabury Press, 1970), p. 44.

15. Dan O. Via, Jr., *Kerygma and Comedy in the New Testament* (Philadelphia: Fortress Press, 1975), p. 46.

16. Wolfhart Pannenberg, *What is Man?: Contemporary Anthropology in Theological Perspective* (Philadelphia: Fortress Press, 1972), Chap. 2.

17. William F. Lynch, *Christ and Apollo: The Dimensions of the Literary Imagination* (New York: Sheed and Ward, 1960), p. 97.

18. Ibid., p. 139.

19. W. H. Auden, *The Collected Poetry of W. H. Auden* (New York: Random House, 1945), p. 454.

20. Lynch, *Christ and Apollo,* p. 107.

CHAPTER EIGHT

Who Suffer and Who Die

Christians reciting the Apostles' Creed make four firm assertions about the man Jesus of Nazareth: he suffered, was crucified, died, and was buried. Those emphatic verbs found their way into the Creed to express the verdict of faith that Jesus was fully and completely human. He was able truly to suffer, truly to die. He was not divinely immune to human pain and human death. He experienced everything that we experience.

Sharing in his humanity, we too must suffer and die. Yet with our characteristic ability to pretend that we are not human, we do our best to hide our own suffering from ourselves, and to put others who are suffering out of sight behind institutional walls. The "huge, macabre and expensive practical joke" on the American public which Jessica Mitford exposed in *The American Way of Death*[1] succeeded because we prefer to hide death, too. The trappings of gracious dying, from satin linings in bronze caskets to wall-to-wall carpeting in the Wee Kirk of the Heather at Forest Lawn Memorial Park, are evidence of the price we are willing to pay to create an illusion of immortality. But underneath we know that we are going to die.

In the last ten years, new questions about the meaning of suffering and death have captured public attention, questions about the human management of human dying. The celebrated case of

105

Karen Quinlan whose breathing was prolonged by machine after she had lost the capacity for human life is just one dramatic symbol of the new situation. Even the traditional criteria for defining death have been called into question. And our current debates about euthanasia as well as about abortion indicate that we have no consensus about the significance of pain and sorrow.

The fact of suffering has haunted the religious imagination since history began; but no one, to my knowledge, has ever come up with a satisfactory answer to the universal question, "Why did this have to happen to *me*?" A grief observed out there is easier to cope with than a grief experienced as my own. It is *my* pain that shakes me most deeply.

Biblical answers to the mystery of suffering are various. Of the four we consider, two of them, in my judgment, must be totally rejected as Christian answers to anyone else's suffering, although they may have some meaning for a better understanding of my own. Two of them have more general application precisely because they are not solutions to a problem but redefinitions of a situation.

The first biblical answer to the sufferer is that God is punishing you for your sins. This understanding is implicit in the Yahwist's account of what happened to Adam and Eve as a result of their disobedience of the divine command. Later theologians in Israel turned this idea of the root of suffering into a formula, and indeed into a philosophy of history. Health, peace, and prosperity are God's reward for righteousness. Sickness, war, and adversity are his just retribution for sin. Eliphaz the Temanite illustrates that all too pat formula in his unfriendly question to Job:

> Think now, who that was
>   innocent ever perished?
> Or where were the upright cut off?
> As I have seen, those who plow iniquity
>   and sow trouble reap the same.

(Job 4:7)

Job was not alone among the ancients who realized that this is just not true to human experience. The author of Psalm 73, for example, saw the prosperity of the wicked, their eyes swollen with fatness, and lamented:

> All in vain have I kept my heart clean
> and washed my hands in innocence.
> For all the day long I have been stricken . . .
>
> (Ps. 73:13–14)

Nevertheless, the idea that suffering and sin are directly connected was still alive in the first century. The Fourth Gospel reports that when Jesus' disciples saw a blind man, they asked him, "Rabbi, who sinned, this man or his parents, that he was born blind?" (John 9:2). Only a slightly less blatant form of the same cruel theory is alive in the twentieth century. Is it through their own fault or through the fault of their mothers on welfare that unemployed ghetto youths get hooked on drugs?

The second biblical understanding of suffering which I believe Christians must flatly reject, at least in relation to other people's suffering, is that God is afflicting them for educational purposes—that suffering is a disciplinary measure used by a loving father, one who beats his children for their own good.

The proverbial wisdom of Israel was strong on not spoiling the child. It decreed that "he who spares the rod hates his son, but he who loves him is diligent to discipline him" (Prov. 13:24). The author of Hebrews picked up on that proverbial wisdom, quoting Proverbs directly, to claim that God disciplines us for our good. It may seem painful for the moment, but "later it yields the peaceful fruit of righteousness to those who have been trained by it" (Heb. 12:11).

Paul evidently shared the conviction that suffering builds character. He invited us to rejoice in our sufferings because they produce endurance, character, and hope (Rom. 5:3–4). This may indeed be true; but I cannot explain things so, in the name of the God of love, to the child with sickle-cell anemia or the victim of torture in the police stations of Latin America.

If we can no longer use the idea of God the Pedagogue to justify misery and encourage masochism, what are the other options for some creative encounter with our own suffering and that of others? The Bible presents us with two different images which better illumine the distress native to our lives. One is best seen in the end of the book of Job. The other is first made explicit in the poetry of Second Isaiah and then enacted in the life of Jesus.

107

In the first instance, the end of the book of Job is ambiguous. Many readers find themselves dissatisfied with what appears to be the final picture—Job the sufferer overwhelmed and silenced by the grandeur of God and the insignificance of man in the cosmos. But this is not the only way to interpret the end of that drama.

After all of Job's demands to be heard, the Lord finally answers him—out of the whirlwind. The divine silence is broken. Job is no longer able to accuse God of indifference or apathy. Indeed God twice insists that Job "gird up his loins like a man" and enter into dialogue with him (38:3; 40:7). "Hear, and I will speak; I will question you, and you declare to me" (42:4). Surely those interpreters are right who find here not a solution to an academic puzzle as to why the innocent suffer, but a new context of relationship in which to confront that experience.[2]

Note that, in wrestling with inexplicable affliction, the poet does not condone silence or apathy on the part either of man or of God. Silence in the face of pain is a Stoic, not a Christian response. As Dorothee Soelle observes in her theological essay on suffering, "To consider the tearless male as an ideal is to acknowledge clearly that nothing is learned from suffering and nothing to be gained from it."[3] Mute suffering needs to find a language of lament in order that it can indict suffering and cry out against it as Job did.

We need to ask two different questions about suffering, Soelle argues. First, what are its causes and how can they be eliminated? Second, under what conditions can suffering make us more human? Passionate crying out against much of the needless suffering in the world is the first step toward changing the situations that can be changed. We need to develop the impatience of Job.

Unfortunately, we get so used to the sufferings around us that we become indifferent to them. Apathy, which originally meant freedom from suffering, has become a synonym for indifference. Apathetic people are afflicted with necrophilia, in Soelle's terms, with a love for that which is "dead, frozen, motionless."[4] There was no apathy in Gethsemane.

In protest against the longstanding theological tradition which held that God is apathetic in the root sense of the word—"without passions" as the English Reformers put it—many theologians today are calling us to become more passionate people, with a com-passionate God. After all, the heart of the New Testament is a passion story.

The double meaning of passion is invoked here. As the term is applied to the New Testament it means all of the sufferings of Jesus from Gethsemane through Golgotha. It also means intense emotion, ardent affection, love. There is a connection between the two. The more we love life and open ourselves to it, Jürgen Moltmann recognizes, the more vulnerable we become. Our ability to love and our ability to suffer are directly dependent on one another. "The more passionately we love life, the more we also experience the pain of life and the deadliness of death."[5]

Soelle makes virtually the same point in answer to her question of the conditions under which suffering can make us more human. Suffering that is accepted and unreservedly affirmed, she believes, has a transforming power. She reached that conclusion after reflecting on the way in which the man Jesus faced the fear of death and made of it a means of strengthening. The affirmation of suffering, however, "is part of the great yes to life as a whole and not, as it sometimes can appear, the sole and decisive affirmation."[6]

Finally, there is another biblical vision of human suffering and its meaning that transcends the ideas of punishment and discipline, and passionate response that we have so far reviewed. It introduces the notion that there is a compassionate "for the sake of" at the heart of human suffering. It asks us to consider, against all logic, that your anguish can help me—just as Jesus' human suffering helped all of us.

Underlying this central Christian insight is a recognition of the intimate interconnectedness of all human life. Since we have lost most of the philosophical presuppositions about the real unity of the human race we have difficulty even beginning to think about the interconnections. Stock words and phrases like "vicarious" and "substituted love" are not much help, nor are most traditional statements of the doctrine of the atonement. Perhaps language which is more obviously metaphoric offers a better starting place. We are all *knit* together in one communion and fellowship. We are all strands in a *web* of glory. Such picturesque language invites us to see how we hold one another together, to see how we hold one another up—in sickness and in health.

Only as we approach this deepest level of the mystery of suffering can we begin to understand what Soelle means when she says that we cannot bear the image of God apart from the image of Christ. That image includes the image of the cross. If we affirm that image, we say goodbye to the "hope of being free of sickness, deformity, and death."[7] But we also open up vistas of new life.

The idea of a redemptive quality in human suffering first appears in biblical thought in the midst of a cycle of poems in Isaiah 40–55 which is generally known as Second Isaiah. In the midst of that great work, to be dated about 550 B.C. when Israel was a subject people in Babylon, are four poems which are called "The Servant Songs." Since 1892 Old Testament scholars have debated the questions of who wrote them and what they mean. They still present immense difficulties to interpreters. But there is no question that the fourth of these songs, Isaiah 52:13—53:12, speaks of affliction in a revolutionary way.

The translation John L. McKenzie, S. J. made for the Anchor Bible offers us a fresh look at the figure known as the Suffering Servant. His disfigurement was so inhuman that "he no longer looked like a man"(Isa. 52:14).

> He was despised, the lowest of men: a man of pains,
>   familiar with disease,
> One from whom men avert their gaze—despised, and we
>   reckoned him as nothing.
> But it was our diseases that he bore, our pains that he
>   carried,
> While we counted him as one stricken, touched by God
>   with affliction.
> He was wounded for our rebellions, crushed for our
>   transgressions;
> The chastisement that reconciled us fell upon him, and
>   we were healed by his bruises.
>
> (Isa. 53:3–5)

Suffering, however undeserved, need not be fruitless, the poet believes. As McKenzie interprets it, the poem says that because this man suffers the pains of others, others are released from pain.[8]

It may be that Jesus himself found in these lines an understanding of his own mission when he set his face to go up to Jerusalem. It is certain, and probably inevitable, that the primitive Christian

community found in them a way to understand Jesus' own sufferings. The author of 1 Peter, for example, uses them to describe
the way in which Christ suffered for us (1 Pet. 2:24). He urges his
hearers to share Christ's sufferings (1 Pet. 4:13). Similarly, Paul
had a profound conviction of the possibility of sharing in Christ's
suffering, and therefore of suffering on behalf of others. His corporate understanding of the body of Christ is such that he can tell
the Corinthian church, "If one member suffers, all suffer together"
(1 Cor. 12:26).

Recently David Baily Harned has argued powerfully that the
image of oneself as a sufferer is one of the master images for self-
recognition, one with possibilities for enrichment of the self. He
rightly distinguishes suffering from pain. Pain may be an element
in suffering, but sometimes "the more complex sorts of suffering
that are the consequences of betrayals of oneself or of others"[9]
have nothing to do with physical pain.

One dimension of this self-understanding is letting things happen to us. The human infant has to allow everything to be done
for it; it comes into life totally dependent on others. The aging
must again accept—suffer—dependence. "Both the self's entrance
into the world and its exit from it are best described as instances
of suffering: this is the essential image."[10]

If we need others most dramatically at birth and death, however,
the case is the same throughout our lives. We are cared for; we
learn to care, to listen to the needs of others, their claims upon us.
There is a reciprocity of giving and receiving which helps make us
human. "The undeserved and pointless suffering that is visited on
others," Harned writes, "can turn us away from ourselves, pierce
the armor of our selfishness, and shatter our carefulness and cal-
culations. . . . "[11] But by the same token, "we need the need that
others have for us, and we become fully personal only in our responsiveness to those needs."[12]

Harned, therefore, proposes that the figure of the sufferer is
the figure of the self's capacity for love. The model of that love
expressed through suffering and for sufferers is Jesus, the suffering servant, the second Adam. The new humanity conformed to
his image affirms the rich possibilities of passion and compassion.

If learning to affirm ourselves as sufferers is ingredient to be-

* "To suffer" in KJV English means "to allow"
or "to permit". ** So Christ is all and in
all according to Paul.

111

coming fully human, so also is learning to affirm ourselves as creatures who die. So remarkable is the upsurge of public interest in death and dying in the last decade that some observers are beginning to sound alarmed, suspecting that it may not be an altogether healthy development. A generation which has the stench of Vietnam as well as of Auschwitz in its nostrils may be showing a morbid fascination with a subject best left in the closet along with other family skeletons. Christian anthropology must be aware of the possible distortions of this as well as every other dimension of selfhood; but between the extremes of genocide and suicide lies a sane acceptance of our own mortality.

Contemporary teachers of the art of dying suggest above all that we learn again to think of death as natural, to admit our oneness with the rest of the created order. They invite us further to think of ourselves as those who live "between the nipple and the everlasting arms."[13] They believe that as we learn to acknowledge death we are freed to celebrate life.

As a modern pioneer in the field, Elisabeth Kübler-Ross has done as much as anyone to reinstruct us in patterns of normality—in what she calls "old-fashioned customs" such as giving the dying patient a glass of wine instead of a sedative, and some home-cooked soup instead of a bottle of intravenous fluids.[14] Her psychological insights into the four necessary stages of denial, anger, bargaining, and depression which precede the final stage of the acceptance of death have made an invaluable contribution to our contemporary self-knowledge. So also has her insistence that these are not neat progressions which each of us follows on schedule.

Another physician who speaks powerfully about that human finitude which links us with every fellow creature from the grasshopper to the elephant is Lewis Thomas. In a brief essay called "Death in the Open," which appeared originally in the *New England Journal of Medicine,* Thomas suggests that the death-denying obsession of American culture and the death-denying compulsion of the human psyche may be of a piece with animal instinct to die in hiding. It is a shock to us when we see a dead animal along the highway or find a dead bird on the lawn, he notes. Animals do their dying off somewhere, behind things, under things. So we forget that "all of the life of the earth dies, all the time, in the same volume as the new life that dazzles us each morning, each spring."[15]

About fifty million human beings die each year in relative secrecy, too. We are aware chiefly of those deaths which affect us personally, and so we look on death as an anomaly. Thomas doubts that we can continue to keep the secret from ourselves as the human population doubles. He thinks we will have to give up the notion that death is a catastrophe or even a stranger. "We will need to learn more about the cycling of life in the rest of the system, and about our connection to the process. Everything that comes alive seems to be in trade for something that dies, cell for cell."[16]

One must raise a question, however, about the idea that we share with other animals a desire to face death alone. The evidence suggests rather that human beings are social beings as well as lonely beings, even in death. Jesus in Gethsemane asked his friends to watch with him. Robert Neale, reporting on six months as a chaplain in London's St. Christopher's Hospice for the terminally ill, remarks on the same desire on the part of the patients.[17] He describes the warm atmosphere of this hospice for travelers on their way to the everlasting arms of God. Being present is what matters most—being present with one another through meals, and through touching and loving. In such an atmosphere people discover that death is All Right.

Picking up on the feminine symbolism present in Neale's account of St. Christopher's, Penelope Washbourn proposed that we stress the similarity between the womb and the tomb by consciously using mother language. "Through the symbol of Mother Earth, the ground of our being, who gave us birth, sustained us and calls us back," she wrote, "death may be experienced not as a threat, but as God's embrace."[18] Perhaps. In my judgment, however, the more important insight she offered for our self-understanding was through her focus on the similarity between love and death. They both involve an ability to let go of control. In human experience and especially in Christian experience, mothers have no monopoly on the gift of love or on the gift of dying well.

One of the best teachers about dying is still the seventeenth-century churchman, John Donne. He deserves a hearing along with more recent writers on the meaning of death for at least three reasons. He recognized more fully than many of the more recent writers that death is a corporate experience, however much we die alone. He was a theologian who saw that all of life is a process of

113

dying. And, because he was a poet, he could speak about death from his imagination to ours. Clinical prose does not have that power.

Donne's biographer, Izaak Walton, tells us that Donne's first sermon after his wife's death was on a text from Lamentations, "I am the man who has seen affliction" (Lam. 3:1). The husband and his wife had both seen affliction. They had buried five of their twelve children before she died. It is well known that Donne had his portrait painted in his own shroud. Less well known, perhaps, is the fact that he also had his portrait painted when he was eighteen. At that time he took as his personal motto, "How much shall I be changed/Before I am changed!" That attitude toward life is undoubtedly one of the reasons why he did not regard death as the King of Terrors, and why Walton could say of his last illness, "And now he was so happy as to have nothing to do but to die, to do which he stood in need of no longer time; for he had studied it long. . . ."[19]

When he was fifty-four Donne became dangerously ill, so ill that he thought the grave was ready to devour him. While he was convalescing from that sickness, Donne wrote the "Devotions" which today's new literature on death often quotes. His meditation on listening to the bells tolling in the church next door expresses his full acceptance of his own mortality, along with his conviction that we share in each other's deaths and lives, whether we want to or not.

> Could I fit myself to stand or sit in any man's place, and not to lie in any man's grave? I may lack much of the good parts of the meanest but I lack nothing of the mortality of the weakest. . . . [20]

Those funeral bells, Donne recognized, meant that a piece of himself was passing out of the world.

> If a clod be washed away by the sea, Europe is the less, as well as if a promontory were, as well as if a manor of thy friend's or of thine own were: any man's death diminishes me, because I am involved in mankind. . . . [21]

The last sermon which this Dean of St. Paul's ever preached was also on the subject of death. The text was from Psalm 68, which in his translation read, "And unto God the Lord belong the issues of death." Throughout the sermon Donne makes it clear how wide a word death is. He speaks of "the manifold deaths" of this world. We "celebrate our own funerals with cries even at our birth."[22] Our deliverance from the death of the womb is an entrance to other deaths—birth dies in infancy, infancy in youth, youth in age. Like St. Paul before him, Donne appropriates death and resurrection as a posture for daily life. Indeed, he speaks not only of every day's but of every hour's death. From this perspective he is able to say, "Our critical day is not the very day of our death, but the whole course of our life."[23]

Shortly before his own death, Donne had some seals and rings designed and engraved as farewell gifts for his friends, among them the poet George Herbert. They bore an image of Christ fixed not to a cross but to an anchor. The triumph of life over death which that symbol of hope expresses is the subject of one of his greatest poems, the tenth of his "Holy Sonnets," which begins "Death be not proud." It ends with the lines:

One short sleepe past, wee wake eternally,
And death shall be no more; death, thou shalt die.[24]

At the beginning of this chapter I stressed the four verbs in the creed of Christendom which underline the full humanity of Jesus. He suffered. He was crucified. He died. He was buried. Those are historical assertions, by anyone's definition. A fifth verbal assertion was omitted, partly because some theologians prefer to think of it as referring to a transhistorical event, but more especially because it must not obscure the verbs which precede it: on the third day *he rose* again.

For John Donne, as for millions of other Christians, the fact of faith—the fact that God raised his Son, Jesus the Christ, on the third day—is the anchor holding human suffering and human death firm in reality. Suffering and death are not meaningless dimensions of human existence, but doors into life.

NOTES

1. Jessica Mitford, *The American Way of Death* (New York: Simon and Schuster, 1963).

2. See, e.g., Samuel Terrien, "Introduction and Exegesis, The Book of Job," *The Interpreter's Bible* (Nashville: Abingdon Press, 1954), Vol. 3, p. 1172.

3. Dorothee Soelle, *Suffering* (Philadelphia: Fortress Press, 1975), p. 125.

4. Ibid., p. 37.

5. Jürgen Moltmann, "The Passion of Life," *Currents in Theology and Mission* 4 (1977): 9.

6. Soelle, *Suffering,* p. 108.

7. Ibid., p. 131.

8. John L. McKenzie, S.J., *Second Isaiah,* The Anchor Bible (New York: Doubleday & Co., 1968), p. 183.

9. David Baily Harned, *Images for Self-Recognition: The Christian as Player, Sufferer, and Vandal* (New York: Seabury Press, 1977), p. 44.

10. Ibid., p. 52.

11. Ibid., p. 49.

12. Ibid., p. 53.

13. Robert E. Neale, "Between the Nipple and the Everlasting Arms," *Union Seminary Quarterly Review* 27 (1972): 81–90.

14. Elisabeth Kübler-Ross, *On Death and Dying* (New York: Macmillan Publishing Co., 1969), p. 6.

15. Lewis Thomas, *The Lives of a Cell: Notes of a Biology Watcher* (New York: Viking Press, 1974), p. 97.

16. Ibid., p. 99.

17. Neale, "Between the Nipple and the Everlasting Arms," pp. 81–90. Cf. his *The Art of Dying* (New York: Harper & Row, 1973).

18. Penelope Washbourn, "Feminine Symbols and Death," *Theology Today* 32 (1975): 248.

19. Izaak Walton, "The Life of Dr. John Donne," reprinted in John Donne, *Devotions upon Emergent Occasions* (Ann Arbor, Mich.: University of Michigan Press, 1959), p. xlvii.

20. Ibid., p. 103.

21. Ibid., pp. 108–109.

22. Donne, "Death's Duel," ibid., p. 170.

23. Ibid., p. 180.

24. John Donne, *Complete Poetry and Selected Prose of John Donne* (New York: Random House, 1941), p. 240.

PART III

Beyond Ourselves

CHAPTER NINE

Our Niche in Nature

"Generations have trod, have trod, have trod . . . the soil is bare now, nor can foot feel, being shod." When Gerard Manley Hopkins composed "God's Grandeur" he had not heard of an environmental crisis. He was able to continue his praise of God's grandeur, "And for all this nature is never spent."

Today we are confronted with damning evidence that nature *can* be spent—used up, worn out or blown up by human beings who have trod the planet with unfeeling feet too long. We react to the facts of the pollution and depletion of our natural resources with the language of "crisis," thereby persuading ourselves that the situation, however painful at the moment, will soon be over. And some of us cart our empty aluminum cans off to recycling centers with some dim sense of atoning for our share in misusing the world around us.

A Christian anthropology in the last quarter of the twentieth century must take into account our new awareness of the precarious state of the biosphere, that thin skin of air, water, and soil which supports all life on this earth. It must ask about human connectedness with sea and sky, newt and shrew, lion and lamb, in terms other than those our ancestors used. Yet in this area also our inherited Scriptures and tradition offer guides to new thought about our human nature.

Four images of our proper relationship with nature will help our thinking: *Mother Earth, the Garden, the Peaceable Kingdom,* and *the City of God.* All have, to one degree or another, a place in biblical understanding of our niche in the world of animate and inanimate things over which we are said to have dominion.

The image of *Mother Earth* is not central to biblical thought. In fact, it can be found explicitly only in one verse from Ecclesiastes, and that in an eccentric translation. The standard description of the rich man's destiny, "As he came from his mother's womb he shall go again, naked as he came" (5:15) becomes, in the New English Bible, "He came from the womb of mother earth." One recent commentator on the resources which the religious imagination can offer for the ecological crisis, however, juxtaposed this verse with Gen. 2:7, where the Adam is formed from the dust of the ground *(adamah),* and confessed:

> ADAMAH, Earth Mother, Mother of Adam, Mother of Man, Mother of birds, of beasts, of herbs and trees, we have wandered far away from you.[1]

Rabbi Everett E. Gendler, who wrote these words in an article called "The Return of the Goddess," was deploring the patriarchal bias of the Hebrew tradition. "To re-claim the matriarchal spirit and our bond with the Earth Mother," he said, "strikes me as necessary if we are to address at all successfully the ecological crisis confronting us."[2]

Throughout Israel's history the Canaanite goddess Ashtoreth was an important rival to Yahweh. Four hundred of her prophets sat at Queen Jezebel's table (1 Kings 18:19). Even King Solomon is indicted for going after her (1 Kings 11:5). Time after time the prophets of Yahweh denounce the fertility cult, and reformers destroy its shrines. The legendary contest on Mount Carmel between Elijah and the rival prophets, which took place in time of drought and famine, dramatizes Israel's conviction that it is the one God who is responsible for the earth's fertility.

There is no clear historical evidence to identify the Canaanite goddess with Mother Earth. She seems to have had closer affinity with the sea. Moreover, the symbol has two other serious limitations which make it an unfortunate choice for imaging forth our human relationship with the rest of nature. First, as is clear to anyone with half an ear for metaphor, it is precisely because we think of the earth as female, consciously or unconsciously, that we are able to speak of "the rape of the planet." Mother Earth may have suffered what she has at the hands of man because of her personification in terms of a sex object.

The rehabilitation of Mother Earth and Mother Nature language, furthermore, could suggest an overdependence on her. Sensing this danger, H. Paul Santmire chose to call his theological study of nature, God, and ecology *Brother Earth.* "From a theological perspective," he notes, "the common parlance 'mother earth' . . . is much too closely tied to the theme of Nature vs. Civilization to be useful any longer."[3] He is also correct in pointing out that our major allegiance is not to nature as such.

Human being emerges on the scene in Genesis 2 in the midst of a garden. The image of *the Garden* as a paradigm for thinking about our proper relationship with the rest of nature has much more to commend it than the image of Mother Earth. Strongly in its favor is the inherent recognition that human being is cultural being, distinguished from the rest of nature by our ability to cultivate. Part of our capacity to be gardeners is our capacity to think creatively. So the garden image calls on our imaginative powers.

Only half in jest, Claude Lévi-Strauss invites us to wonder whether Adam and Eve cooked in the Garden of Eden. He has observed that just as no human society can exist without language, so no human society can exist without cooking. Eating (and not eating) are certainly important matters in the Yahwist's creation account (Genesis 2), but the implication is that the menu was fruit and nuts. Human beings seem to have been thought of as vegetarians until after the Flood, when Noah and his family are given divine permission to eat meat also (Gen. 9:3). Be that as it may, our ability to process food is basic to our humanity.

Think for a moment, as Edmund Leach asks us to do,[4] about oysters, smoked salmon, and Stilton cheese. These represent raw, processed, and rotten foods, a culinary triangle which Lévi-Strauss analyzed as one of the universal structures of human society. They also represent the complexity of our relationship to nature. To survive we have to eat; we do not have to cook. But cooking is one of the symbolic activities whereby all human societies distinguish

120

themselves from animals. And today, most of our foodstuffs, even the raw oysters, are cultivated. We are put in the garden, according to Genesis, "to till it and keep it" (2:15).

Fashions in gardening change, just as styles of cooking do. Our way of gardening is also a profoundly symbolic act. The change from the clipped formal gardens of the seventeenth century to the so-called English garden popular everywhere in the eighteenth century foreshadowed a change in understanding the universe. Arthur O. Lovejoy made this point years ago in his classic study of the history of an idea, *The Great Chain of Being:*

> In one of its aspects that many-sided thing called Romanticism may not inaccurately be described as an *englischer Garten* on a grand scale. The God of the seventeenth century, like its gardeners, always geometrized; the God of Romanticism was one in whose universe things grew wild and without trimming and in all the rich diversity of the natural shapes.[5]

The current popularity of organic gardening may presage another great change in the way we look at the universe, but it is well to note the similarities between some of the present day nature mysticism and that of the earlier romanticism. Preservation of wilderness areas is undoubtedly important, but for the sake of human beings. Christians cannot fully agree with Henry David Thoreau's dictum that the preservation of the world depends on wilderness.

Central to current theological debate about our place in nature is the critical text with which we began our study: "Then God said, "Let us make man in our image, after our likeness; and let them have dominion over the fish of the sea, and over the birds of the air, and over the cattle, and over all the earth. . . ." (Gen 1:26) Some charge that this text has been used as a warrant for suicidal emphasis on the superiority of human beings in the natural order. Others think that human dominion over creation is imperative for God's sake and our own. The question becomes, "How loudly should a Christian say that human beings are unique?"

Earlier Christian theologians accepted unquestioningly the idea of human dominion over fish and fowl as a facet of the image of God. One of them, Diodore of Tarsus, put it succinctly: "How, then, is man God's image? By way of dominion, in virtue of authority."[6] Most of his fellow theologians in the early centuries of

121

the church agreed with him that human beings have a divinely allotted sovereignty over all other creatures of the earth. They stressed the radical difference between man and beast, our God-given imperial power to collect tribute from earth and sea. One of the reasons human beings are said to be in the image of God, they were convinced, is that they are "earth's sovereign."

For centuries this apparently unmitigated anthropocentrism was counterbalanced in Christian thought, however, by two other powerful ideas. People believed also that there were innumerable beings higher than humanity in God's great chain of being. They believed at the same time that they were God's stewards, his gardeners on this earth. The chain-of-being motif may no longer be available to limit human arrogance, but the stewardship motif has strong champions today.

When people were persuaded, as even John Locke was in the eighteenth century, "that there are far more species of creatures above us, than there are beneath,"[7] their sense of cosmic importance was kept in check. The claim that the world was made for the sake of humanity, "that it might serve him," was offset by the belief, however contradictory, that the great variety of species existed not to serve people, but to show forth the plenitude of *being* in a complete series of all possible forms. When human beings thought of themselves as the middle link in such a chain, they knew not only that they were just a little lower than the angels, but also that they were just a little higher than the next animal. They were less likely to separate themselves from their next of kin. They realized, as Alexander Pope did a century before Darwin, that

> Man walk'd with beast, joint tenant of the shade;
> The same his table, and the same his bed.[8]

It is hard for a historian to agree with Loren Eisley that Darwin's demonstration of our physical relationship with the world of lower animals was "one of the most dreadful blows that the human ego has ever sustained."[9]

Human dominion over other creatures, both animals and plants, was also limited in biblical thought by the idea that we are caretakers of God's creation. That role is beautifully expressed in *The Book of Common Prayer* psalter (1979):

The heaven of heavens is the Lord's,
   but he entrusted the earth to its peoples.

(Ps. 115:16)

We are stewards of God's bounty, holding creation in trust. New Testament parables often present the picture of God as an absentee landowner, accounting his stewards responsible for the welfare of his vineyards. The language has a reference beyond that of good farming, but the idea of responsibility for the welfare of the earth is surely included.

Writing on the purpose for which human beings were created, a seventeenth-century churchman argued that they were to be "Farmers of this goodly Farm of the lower World." We were invested with dominion, trust, and care "to preserve the *Species* of diverse Vegetables, to improve them and others, to correct the redundance of unprofitable Vegetables, to preserve the face of the Earth in beauty, usefulness, and fruitfulness."[10] Such an attitude toward our planet is far from the ruthless defacing of nature which some contemporary conservationists blame directly on the biblical charge to subdue the earth.

There is another aspect of the image of a garden which must be noted. While describing Eden the Yahwist said, "And out of the ground the Lord God made to grow every tree that is pleasant to the sight and good for food. . . ." (Gen. 2:9) He puts beauty first. When we think of our relationship to nature in terms of a garden, we are invited to contemplate beauty—to enjoy the sight of a seagull in flight, the song of a wren, the smell of sun on pine needles, the taste of strawberries, the feel of sand between our toes. We are called to stand in awe and wonder beneath a redwood tree, to delight in the ginkgo trees that grow along Broadway, to marvel at snowflake and thunderstorm, penguin and porcupine. Paul Santmire aptly calls this aspect of our relation to nature that of "wondering onlooker."

With all of its strength as a model for expressing a right relationship with nature, nonetheless the garden-gardener image has serious limitations which need to be corrected by two other biblical images. It is absurdly easy to sentimentalize our relation to a garden; we need the eschatological symbol of *the Peaceable Kingdom* to remind us, among other things, that in nature, cats eat birds and

123

mosquitoes bite. It is also easy, if we think only in garden terms, to look back instead of forward, to yearn for the Amazon jungle in place of the asphalt jungle, to deplore technology and to despise those who like plastic better than wood. We need the eschatological symbol of *the City of God* to remain Christian realists.

Nature as we know it is not all bunny rabbits. It is dangerous and frightening as well as beautiful and wonder-making. Thomas Derr helps us see through our modern nature-romanticism when he notes the fraudulent and comic aspects of the annual camping trip accompanied by insect bombs and bottled gas—"a rolling bit of city running through nature's hostile territory on the pretext of enjoying it, but secretly scarcely able to wait for the next motel and its hot shower."[11] Derr believes that we are continually made human by asserting our distinction from other animals. To emphasize complete oneness with nature is a threat to humanness.

The ambiguity of our relationship with the animal kingdom is also clearly seen by both Lévi-Strauss and the prophet Isaiah. One of the anthropologist's major works was on totemism. One of his central preoccupations has been to explore the dialectical process by which our apotheosis of ourselves as other than animal is "formed and re-formed and bent back upon itself."[12] He continues this interest in another of his major works, translated under the misleading title *The Savage Mind*.[13] He makes it quite clear that he sees no distinction in principle between the thought of so-called primitive people about animals and that of the zoologist who currently directs the Zurich zoo.

Lévi-Strauss asks us to reflect on our complex relationship with animals by considering the different ways in which we name birds and dogs and racehorses and cattle. In the West we give dogs personal names and have a taboo against eating them. Cattle, in our culture, are more overtly treated as objects rather than subjects, since they are part of our technical and economic system. In the cattle cultures of Africa, things are reversed. And in cultures where one belongs to the clan of Bear or Beaver or Eagle the details differ, but the structures do not.

A group of illustrations in the middle of the book *The Savage Mind* vividly demonstrates the strangeness of our relationship with other animals. It reproduces caricatures of men and women look-

124

ing like owls and foxes and sheep, on the one hand, and of humanized nature, with birds dressed up as people, on the other. The effect is the same if you think both of the greeting cards people buy showing Mrs. Mouse sweeping out her house, and of cartoons which turn some political leader into a ravenous lion seeking someone to devour.

Human beings, that is, recognize their elementary kinship with animals and their estrangement from them. Edith Wharton captured that dual relationship when she wrote, "I am secretly afraid of animals—of all animals except dogs, and even of some dogs. I think it is because of the *us-ness* in their eyes, with the underlying *not-usness* which belies it."[14]

The prophet Isaiah long ago foresaw a day when that age-old fear of animals will be overcome, a day indeed when children can safely play with rattlesnakes. Not only will the enmity between human beings and snakes be overcome in that day, but wild and domestic animals will be reconciled to each other. The great eschatological vision in Isa. 11:6–9 is remarkable for its linking of the not-tamed and the tamed. The enmity between bear and cow, wolf and lamb, leopard and goat, lion and ox will come to an end. A new harmony will prevail in nature because "the earth shall be full of the knowledge of the Lord as the waters cover the sea" (Isa. 11:9).

The well-known paintings of that vision of a *Peaceable Kingdom*[15] by the nineteenth-century American Quaker signpainter and preacher, Edward Hicks, delight some contemporary environmentalists. Although they have come down to us in several versions, the paintings all portray adult human beings down in the lower corner, where William Penn talks with the Indians. The center of the stage is taken over by the lion and the ox—and the little child. The paintings therefore counteract the anthropocentrism which some environmentalists believe has put us on the endangered species list along with the wolf.

For Christian theology, however, that vision of Isaiah has long been understood as pointing forward to the unity of all creation restored in Jesus Christ. It speaks of a peace in the animal kingdom of which we are a part, not only in terms of new knowledge of the Creator, but also of new leadership. The interconnectedness of the

*Won't we be surprised to find what creatures God has chosen to share his 'Heaven!

125

whole creation which the passage emphasizes is the same interconnectedness which Paul recognized in his letter to the Romans: "We
know that the whole creation has been groaning in travail together
until now" (8:22). But at the same time he could say, "The creation
itself will be set free from its bondage to decay and obtain the
glorious liberty of the children of God" (8:21).

The invitation which *the Peaceable Kingdom* imagery offers, if you
will, is an ecological one in the dictionary sense of the term. It asks
us to think about the interrelationships of organisms and their
environment. It asks us to believe that human destiny affects the
destiny of cow and bear. It is also an invitation to hope. But it is
not an invitation to sentimentalize beastly behavior or to underestimate the importance of human beings on this globe.

The issue of whether human beings really belong in the center
of the canvas is hotly contested by contemporary theologians trying
to rethink our relationship with nature in order to arrive at a
responsible Christian view of the ecological crisis. Derr, for example, makes the strong statement that our bond to our fellow
human beings is stronger than our bond to the rest of nature.[16]
He believes that ecology is in fact always a question of human
ecology, because we obviously know nothing of an undisturbed
nature in which to seek our niche.

Santmire, on the other hand, objects to Derr's implicit belief that
nature is simply a stage for human beings, the scenery for human
history. He thinks that in the eyes of God nature has independent
value apart from humanity, that God loves alligators and wishes
their fulfillment as well as yours and mine. He is fearful that efforts
to work out a responsible theology of dominion will inevitably turn
into a theology of domination. He asks, "Is it somehow threatening
to our sense of importance on little planet earth to think that God
also is working out God's purposes with the galaxies as well as with
us?"[17]

Appeal to outer space to keep human self-definition in perspective has been with us ever since Copernicus. Already in the six-
teenth century we were entertaining the idea that other planets of
our solar system are inhabited by rational creatures and that
planets in other systems have conscious inhabitants as well. The
space age was not the first to question theological anthropocentrism either. A sixteenth-century poet asked, "It is not blasphe-
126

mous to say that the heavens are a desert and rejoice in no residents, and that God rules only over us and the beasts?"[18]

Between a Star Trek theology and a Back-to-Nature theology, it seems to me, we must set the biblical picture of the new heaven and the new earth—in the shape of a new Jerusalem. The image of *the City* complements the images of *the Garden* of Eden and of *the Peaceable Kingdom* by affirming the fact that the dwelling of God *is* with human beings, by affirming fabricated nature, and also by affirming the value of a river "bright as crystal" (Rev. 22:1).

To elaborate the last point first and most briefly, *the City of God* described in the last pages of Christian Scripture should delight any nature lover's heart. There the city street is lined with trees— or is it just one tree spanning the sacred river? Photographic clarity of detail is not possible when human beings try to describe what life might be like. But this portrait clearly realizes the healing powers of a leafy environment and of clean water. Natural symbols are necessary to express the seer's faith in human destiny. We remain inhabitants of nature.

Nevertheless, however much it is a garden city, *the City of God* of which the Book of Revelation speaks is an urban development whose architectural features can be surveyed and measured. We are asked to think of our future not only in an environment of trees and rivers, but in the company of nature as it has been transformed by human hands. We are to be wondering onlookers not only at Orion and the Pleiades, but also at the Golden Gate Bridge, Chartres Cathedral, and the Bach B Minor Mass. Our relation to nature and its beauty includes our relation to steel cables, sculptured stone, and disciplined sound—and to nuclear reactors and computers as well.

When we think about our connections with the natural world today, it is essential to include technology as a component in that world. One physicist argued not long ago that only in an age capable of producing a sophisticated technology are we able to have a relationship with our environment which can approach that of an I-Thou relationship, because technology frees us from so many fears and terrors of the night.[19] As over against undue pessimism or undue optimism about technological achievements, he urged recognition of technology's humanizing possibilities.

A similar point of view was expressed by John Black, Professor

127

of Natural Resources at the University of Edinburgh, when he insisted that "the only remedy for the misuse of techniques for the management of nature is the adoption of further and more advanced techniques."[20] Both scientists ask us to face the fact that we do not live in a static world of nature, but in one in which technological intervention is inescapable, and on an increasingly massive basis.

Such an affirmation of a technological world is by no means an affirmation of the machine as master. It is fully consonant with the call for a different kind of technology, "a technology with a human face," one gentle in its use of scarce resources and designed to serve human persons.[21] Yet it is a realistic rather than a romantic view of the future, and a realistic rather than a romantic view of how human being fits into the universe.

We are called forward in biblical imagery to a *City,* a *polis.* We are called forward to give thanks for the blazing fact that, for us and for our salvation, God incarnate suffered outside the city. And we are thereby called to exercise responsible dominion over that nature in which we are imbedded.

We will do well to think of ourselves as gardeners in Eden. But it is imperative also for us to think of ourselves as citizens, citizens who have a vote as to how technology will be used to build the cities and the kingdoms of the future.

NOTES

1. Rabbi Everett E. Gendler, "The Return of the Goddess," in *Ecology: Crisis and New Vision,* R. E. Sherrill, ed., (Atlanta: John Knox Press, 1971), p. 134.

2. Ibid., p. 143.

3. H. Paul Santmire, *Brother Earth* (New York: Thomas Nelson, 1970), note p. 228.

4. Edmund Leach, *Claude Lévi-Strauss* (New York: Penguin Books, 1976), Chap. 2.

5. Arthur O. Lovejoy, *The Great Chain of Being* (Cambridge, Mass.: Harvard University Press, 1936), p. 16.

6. Diodore of Tarsus, as quoted by Walter J. Burghardt, *The Image of God in Man According to Cyril of Alexandria* (Washington, D.C.: Catholic University of America Press, 1957), p. 60.

7. John Locke, *Essay Concerning Human Understanding* III, as quoted by Lovejoy, *Chain of Being,* p. 190.

8. Quoted by Lovejoy, *Chain of Being*, pp. 196–197.

9. Loren Eisley, *The Immense Journey* (New York: Random House, 1957), p. 157.

10. Matthew Hale, *The Primitive Origination of Mankind* as quoted by John Black, *The Dominion of Man* (Edinburgh: Edinburgh University Press, 1970), p. 56.

11. Thomas Sieger Derr, *Ecology and Human Liberation* (London: World Student Christian Federation, 1973), p. 37.

12. Leach, *Lévi-Strauss*, p. 36.

13. Claude Lévi-Strauss, *The Savage Mind* (Chicago: University of Chicago Press, 1966).

14. Edith Wharton, as quoted by Kenneth Clark, *Animals and Men* (New York: William Morrow & Co., 1977), p. 51.

15. See Edward Hicks, *A Peaceable Season* (Princeton, N.J.: Pyne Press, 1973); introduction by Eleanore Price Mather.

16. Derr, *Ecology*, p. 11.

17. H. Paul Santmire, "Ecology and Ethical Ecumenics," *Anglican Theological Review* 59 (1977): 100.

18. Palingenius, *Zodiacus Vitae*, as quoted by Lovejoy, *Chain of Being*, p. 115.

19. William H. Klink, "Environmental Concerns and the Need for a New Image of Man," *Zygon* 9 (1974): 300–310.

20. Black, *The Dominion of Man*, p. 126.

21. E. F. Schumacher, *Small is Beautiful* (New York: Harper & Row, 1973), p. 145.

* My pessimistic view of human beings prevents me from holding any such view as remotely possible. Population & economic pressures along with political tensions and means of mass destruction virtually insure the downfall of any such noble visions of the future. We are in the bare infancy of technology as a force affecting life and we have no basis for believing that any life at all will exist 200 or 2000 years from now.

CHAPTER TEN

Rooted in History

New awareness of the precarious state of our natural environment, with all the questions about the future that it raises, is curiously linked with new awareness in this decade of our need for roots in the past. To learn that almost seven hundred years ago someone complained to King Edward I that the once pure water of the Thames was "sore decayed" by the filth of tanners somehow helps us to interpret our own experience. To read in a 1661 diary that the cloud of "sea-coale" perpetually over London is "so universally mixed with the otherwise wholesome and excellent *Aer,* that her *Inhabitants* breathe nothing but an impure and thick mist"[1] somehow helps our self-understanding today. Just what does a historical perspective contribute to our being human in the present?

Polluted water in fourteenth-century London and polluted air in seventeenth-century London may tempt us to think that there is nothing new under the sun, that human nature does not change. It will be our purpose in this chapter to see how Christian understanding of human selfhood as immersed in history offers, on the contrary, a dynamic mode of transcending our own times and our own time, opening us to the future with its promise of a new earth. In order to move forward, we need to behave like Lot's wife and look back. But instead of having a paralyzing effect, looking backward can mobilize us for a thrust forward.

"History" is an elastic word. We use it very loosely in everyday speech. It can refer to what happened long ago. Depending on how old you are, anyone from King Tut to King Kong can qualify for a role in such "ancient history." It can refer just as well to the world of our grandparents' day, when a pound of coffee cost nineteen cents. But we also use the word "history" to speak of our own past—of our childhood and adolescent experiences, of our medical or military records. In each context, therefore, we need to ask questions about the meaning of the word. How can we put together all these strata of our history?

Writing about "Man as History," Wolfhart Pannenberg claims that historical science is the "crown of all anthropological sciences" because of its concreteness.[2] We will try to illustrate the truth of that claim as we think about *biblical history, social history,* and *personal history*—three major roots which help us grow.

Biblical history—for some the phrase immediately conjures up dreary lists in Genesis of who begat whom, or the monotonous formulas of the Books of the Kings, such as "In the twelfth year of Ahaz king of Judah Hoshea the son of Elah began to reign in Samaria over Israel, and he reigned nine years" (2 Kings 17:1). The history I ask you to think about, on the contrary, gives us an account of real women and real men changing the future. It concerns not only a small group of people living at the eastern end of the Mediterranean, but the whole drama of world history. And it confronts us with the claim that God is the sovereign Lord of history who has inaugurated its End. To explicate those assertions we will look at just three concrete events of the past, events through which a woman named Rahab, a man named Cyrus, and a man named Jesus altered your life and mine.

The first event, the one in which Rahab is the heroine, is presented to us by Israel's historians with abundant concrete detail in the second chapter of the Book of Joshua. When Joshua sent two advance spies into the ancient city of Jericho, Rahab "the harlot" took them up on the roof and hid them under stalks of flax that she was drying there. She told the king's police that the spies had already escaped from the city the night before. Subsequently she let them down on a rope out of her city wall window. Before they left they arranged with her to hang a scarlet cord out of the same

131

window at the time of the forthcoming invasion, so that the troops would know which household to spare.

In later biblical tradition Rahab thus becomes an example of one of the pioneers of faith (Heb. 11:31), and an example of one of the pioneers of good works (James 2:25). According to Matthew's genealogy, a woman named Rahab was one of Jesus' forebears— although no one is certain that she was the same woman as Rahab "the harlot."

If we look at this alleged event of the past with the hard eyes of a critical historian, it is clear that no one can demonstrate that this "really happened" in the way the report says that it did. As far as I know, there is no extrabiblical evidence bearing on this particular citizen of the ancient city of Jericho. So Rahab reminds us of the problematic character of all our reconstructions of past events, from the time of Israel's occupation of Canaan and before, to the current historian telling us how and why one candidate won the American presidency and the other lost.

Those three types of questions—what happened? how did it happen? why did it happen?—are all inseparable parts of the major question we ask of the past, "How did we get where we are?" The answer to any one of them always has an element of uncertainty about it.

Another way of approaching the issue of what "history" means is to ask about the status of historical "fact" and historical "myth" in shaping our self-understanding in the present. Many nineteenth-century historians, taking their cue from the natural sciences, were concerned to discover the facts of the past, much as one could discover by empirical observation the mating habits of the woodcock. Prototype of such historians was Leopold von Ranke who, as a professor of history in Berlin in 1825, undertook to uncover the past "as it really happened." His modern counterpart is the television detective who announces that all he wants is the facts. In the case of Rahab, a decisive coup for such an historian would be to discover, say, an ancient potsherd so inscribed as to support the tradition that Rahab was not a harlot, after all, but rather an innkeeper.

Since the early part of the twentieth century, however, historians have overwhelmingly repudiated this view of their task and its underlying assumptions about what is important to know. Often

132

cited as an early spokesman for this newer breed of historians is the American Carl Becker. He recognized the futility of the effort to collect all the facts and then let them "speak for themselves." First, it is impossible to gather *all* of the facts about any event. Second, even if one could, Becker said, "the miserable things wouldn't say anything, would say just nothing at all."[3] As early as 1910 Becker told readers of *The Atlantic Monthly* that historians are "of that ancient and honourable company of the tribe . . . to whom in successive ages has been entrusted the keeping of the useful myths."[4]

Theologians in recent years have suggested a view of history similar in many respects to Becker's. Thus, W. Taylor Stevenson, for example, considering *History as Myth*, defines history as "a way of ordering the totality of human experience in which ultimate or sacral meaning is understood to be present in empirical and transitory phenomena."[5] He agrees with R. G. Collingwood that any disjunction of fact and interpretation in that unity we call history is a fallacy. What Rahab did and how both Israelites and Christians interpreted it are all of a piece.

A similar plea for a unitive view of fact and interpretation, for recognition of an interdependence between events and perceiving minds, was presented in a more recent article with a new twist in the title, "The Release of History through Myth." Like Becker, Stevenson, Collingwood, and others before him, the author, James B. Wiggins, realizes that fact does not equal reality. Rather, historical thought, as he understands it, is essential to the human capacity to imagine reality; history is a key to unlock "the symbolic richness of events" and allow them "to be deepened with expressions of real experience."[6] History cannot be reduced to a book of factual lists such as one finds in *The World Almanac* or the Guinness *Book of World Records*.

Biblical historians are likely to agree that the event of Rahab befriending Joshua's spies unlocks a symbolic richness, but not all of them can abandon lightly the question of whether it was a "real" historical experience. It would be nice to know more about Rahab, more about her motives and her actions than we do or probably ever can. Such matters are not totally unimportant to Christian faith, a faith which interprets history with sacred seriousness. The story of Rahab is part of a larger picture, however; and that is why

133

Cyrus the Great, who built the largest empire known to the ancient world, commands our attention.

Cyrus shares with Rahab one important characteristic in our mythic reconstruction of historical reality. Both are non-Israelites. But Cyrus adds even more than Rahab to the symbolic richness of events because we have relatively greater certainty about his human experience and also contemporary evidence of how Israel interpreted his actions.

Cyrus, you may recall, was the brilliant military leader from southern Iran who, in 550 B.C., took over the vast Empire of the Medes and then swept across Asia to conquer most of what is now Turkey. In 539, he made a triumphant entrance into the city of Babylon where the Jews were living in "captivity." By 538 he controlled all of western Asia to the Egyptian border. As part of his generous imperial policy toward subject peoples, he not only allowed the exiled Jews to return to their homeland, but gave them considerable cultural autonomy there.

In stressing the fact that both Rahab and Cyrus were not members of the tribes of Israel, I wish to recognize the limitations of viewing all of history as the history of God's dealings with his chosen people. Although that is a primary ordering of reality which biblical thought proposes to our imaginations, Cyrus and Rahab tell us that God is interested not only in the so-called Western world. They tell us that all human history is of a piece, even in this most pluralistic of ages.

It has been fashionable for a number of years to describe the Bible as a collection of writings presenting a view of history as *Heilsgeschichte*, "holy history." The chief story line in human events concerns God's relationship with the Israelites and their Christian heirs, the self-styled New Israel. There is much merit in the term and the concept, but recent critics have rightly called attention to two serious limitations.

An exclusive emphasis on the Bible as a record of holy history, as "the book of the acts of God," left a false impression of its contents. It seemed to ignore the large number of biblical writings which are short story and law and proverbs and songs of praise and love poetry. It tended to reduce the multiplicity of literary genres in Scripture to the single category of history, however holy,

134

and thereby tended, necessarily, to distort the ways God makes himself known in human life.

Even more serious, however, was the way in which the category *Heilsgeschichte* appeared to separate some history, a relatively small piece of history, from the vast majority of events on the face of the globe. It led Christians to a reinforced tunnel vision—one which saw God active in the lives of Abraham, Isaac, and Jacob, George Washington, John Adams, and John Kennedy. It left out of view and out of account what God was doing with the Mayans and the Malaysians, with the Bantus and the Bushmen, with Cleopatra and Catherine the Great. As W. Taylor Stevenson argues persuasively in his critique of the notion of *Heilsgeschichte,* it can fragment our world by making a fundamental distinction—basically unbiblical—between ordinary history and special history, profane and sacred history. In biblical thought about history, the affairs of Israel are essentially interwoven with those of Egypt, Assyria, Babylon, Persia, Greece, and Rome.

The great poet "Second Isaiah," to whom we listened when we were thinking about suffering, is the one who tells us most vividly that God is the Lord of universal history, that he uses emperors as well as harlots to serve his purposes. It was Second Isaiah, writing in all probability on the eve of Cyrus's entry into Babylon, who said:

> Thus says the Lord to his anointed, to Cyrus,
>   whose right hand I have grasped,
> to subdue nations before him
>   and ungird the loins of kings, . . .
> I will go before you . . .
>
> I call you by your name,
>   I surname you, though you do not know me.
> I am the Lord, and there is no other. . . .
>
> (Isa. 45:1–2,4–5)

Along with this ringing assertion of God's rule over all of history, Second Isaiah also asserted as emphatically as any of the prophets that human history is a realm where *new* things happen. Just as Cyrus was about to change the whole course of the future, the poet called on his people to sing a new song. In the name of the Lord, he declared:

135

> Behold, the former things have come to pass,
> and new things I now declare.
>
> (Isa. 42:9)

Each historical event has a radical newness about it. Unrepeatable actions of men and women in time are the stuff of history. When Jesus was born in Judea in the reign of Caesar Augustus he entered into a concrete historical existence. He was, as Paul reminds us, born of woman, born under the law. He had his own genealogy, was heir of his own family tradition. He was heir of a religious tradition. And he himself thought historically; he made judgments about the past and acted in light of those judgments.

All human beings think historically, not just the professionals who do research and write books about the past. Van Harvey illustrated that point nicely by describing historical thought as what a parent does in trying to discover which of the children is telling the truth about who put the crayon marks on the bedroom wall.[7] We seek out the truth of the past in the perplexity of present situations. We make decisions about the truth and act in the light of them.

Jesus, in his particular individual human life, did the same. The Gospel of Luke, with its report of Jesus decisively putting his childhood behind him when he was twelve, sitting in the temple among the teachers listening and asking them questions, suggests this with symbolic richness. Questioning the past and learning from it are underlined again in Luke's report of Jesus' sermon in Nazareth. Luke, often described as a theologian of history, is also the evangelist who tells us that Jesus "set his face to go to Jerusalem" (9:51).

The Christian community has always understood itself as a community brought into being by that trip Jesus decided to take to Jerusalem and the cross. No major historical event is completely past. You and I are what we are partly because Caesar crossed the Rubicon, the Pilgrims crossed the Atlantic, Washington crossed the Delaware, and the astronauts went to the moon. But the decision that the historical Jesus made in conversation with the past of his people was, Christians believe, a major historical event which both judges history and transforms it. They find in it a paradigmatic event for interpreting their own present. They believe it ushered in a *new age* which is moving toward the fulfillment of God's purpose in history.

136

Human selfhood before God is historical selfhood, we have been saying. It counts on the past to help shape its self-understanding in the present. It depends on accounts of the past to recognize the possibilities of tomorrow. Yet history has to be rewritten in every generation because our perspectives change. We need to ask new questions of the past. And new history must be made.

We can get out of our own skins and relate to our goodly heritage in biblical faith by focusing on such individuals as Rahab and Cyrus and Jesus, agents of change and accessories before the fact that we are who we are today. We can also stretch ourselves, go beyond ourselves, as we enter spaces of our common past which many of us have never visited.

In this generation we have been dramatically reminded of the need to rewrite history so that it includes more of the human race than Western culture has traditionally included in its narratives of significant events. If we are to understand each other today we must know more about native American experience, black experience, and the experience of many additional ethnic groups. *Social history* seeks to remember, to celebrate, and to learn from all of our predecessors on this planet—ordinary people as well as heroes. In this context the word "history" evokes a wide-angle lens. We need to know that we are treading where all the saints have trod.

Writing about her own grandparents, who in her terms were "people of color," Pauli Murray captured the urgency of such a widening of historical perspective in her superb title, *Proud Shoes.* The titles of two other contemporary efforts to remove historical blinders are much less self-affirming—*Not in God's Image,*[9] which is a history of women in Europe, and *The Underside of History: A View of Women Through Time.*[10] The history of women illustrates our need to appropriate as fully as possible our shared human past, our social history. Many scholars are doing fresh historical research on the subject of women. As a result we are all newly able to light up some of the hitherto dark corners of the past and therefore to see more clearly where we have all come from.

As women search for a usable past, they are discovering and republishing buried treasures. One example is *The Woman's Bible,* an 1890s commentary written by a committee of women under the leadership of Elizabeth Cady Stanton. Her remarkably balanced comment on Rahab gives the flavor of that work:

137

From the text and what we know of humanity in general, it is difficult to decide Rahab's real motive, whether to serve the Lord by helping Joshua to take the land of Canaan, or to save her own life and that of her kinsmen. It is interesting to see that in all national emergencies, leading men are quite willing to avail themselves of the craft and cunning of women, qualities uniformly condemned when used for their own advantage.[11]

When Stanton's work was first published, let it be noted, the Hartford *Seminary Record* called it "the most humorous book of the year."[12]

Collective movements among women have always been ridiculed. The Women's Christian Temperance Union is a clear case in point. The historian Gerda Lerner has brought together a number of documents from the American past under the title *The Female Experience*.[13] Her selection of texts from diaries, letters, periodicals, and personal memoirs poignantly shows how it feels to be the object of derision. It also shows that periods of history regarded as "progressive" for men have often been regressive for women. The affluence of the "self-made" American male is seen to be closely tied to the increasingly passive-dependent and often neurasthenic "lady of leisure."

Most important, perhaps, the book establishes as fact, with documentation, that today's so-called "women's movement" has been with us throughout our history, although never in monolithic form. Reviewing the book for the *New York Times,* Adrienne Rich concluded, "To grasp this as a primary historical reality is to transform the values by which history has been ordered; it is also to shatter the parochialism of here and now, the uninformed belief that 'the' women's movement of today is a passing fad or a marginal phenomenon."[14]

Women have been virtually ignored as participants in Christian history as well as in the rest of world history. As recently as 1965, for example, a history of the Episcopal Church in the United States, one intended to provide a detailed interpretation of some two centuries of the life of that denomination, listed in the relatively complete index just one woman. Her name? The Virgin Mary.

Anonymity for half of the population reinforced a distorted view of the church's past, of course; but it also made it difficult for both

women and men, sisters and brothers in Christ, to know what it
means to be human in the present. Until such time as we pass
beyond the efforts to compensate for invisibility which are represented by books devoted just to "women of the Bible," "women in
Christian tradition," "women in the Church," we cannot fully know
what it means to be created in the image of God, male and female.
Indeed, until women become visible in the mainstream of history,
none of us, male or female, can achieve that richer understanding
of selfhood before God which is the concern of Christian anthropology.

Nevertheless, in this transitional period, extra attention to the
lives of women is helping to give us keener insight into social history, and especially our current history. The works of Robert and
Jane Hallowell Coles demonstrate this fact. Their sensitive accounts of the lives of *Women of Crisis,*[15] which they call lives of
struggle and hope, lives of work and dreams, make their readers
mindful of the great variety of people in this country, and of the
complexities of racial history and class history, as well as of gender
history, which make us who we are. From Appalachia to Alaska
women and men have a great deal in common. The struggles and
dreams of factory workers are akin to the struggles and dreams of
migrant farm workers. We share a common story.

But each of us has her or his own *personal story* to tell as well.
Although our uniqueness as individuals has already been highlighted in earlier chapters, we need to think further about that
uniqueness. How can we tell individual life stories, how can we use
autobiography to help discover our own identity? Each of us is
shaped not only by biblical history and social history, but also by
a *personal history,* distinctive and nonrepeatable. In this recounting
of our story, as well as in the others, the process involves not only
reciting the data but interpreting them. Storytelling is an art, never
an exact science.

Currently theologians are expressing great interest in learning
to tell one's own life story, and learning to tell it well—if only to
ourselves. Judging from some of the best examples of the art, good
autobiography has the same qualities as good storytelling of any
kind.

This means, first, that good autobiography focuses on significant
events, events which had an impact on one's own inner being and

139

becoming. A life story is not the same as a resume, which lists date and place of birth, marital status, education and degrees, jobs held, clubs joined. It is not like an entry in *Who's Who*. Rather it is, by nature, episodic. One thinks of Augustine telling us what happened to him in a garden near Milan during a spring vacation from his teaching job one year. Or recounting what occurred when he was standing with his mother by an open window in Ostia, before sailing back to his home in North Africa. Such events change and shape lives.

Second, such events need not be dramatic, revolutionary events of the magnitude we associate with St. Augustine's "conversion." They can be little, mundane, one-day events which no one else knew about or cared about at the time. I am reminded of that Christmas day Lincoln Steffens remembered from his childhood—an unforgettable day in the life of a small boy, waiting and waiting for the promised pony that had not yet come down the road. Or again of the evening Gandhi recalled, when he was invited out for dinner during his youth as a student in England and was served rare roast beef. For both men, looking back, these experiences contributed to lifelong attitudes and expectations, and to self-understanding.

Sometimes we don't recognize the import of an event when it happens. Sam Keen tells well the story of a peachseed monkey he saw his father carving one summer's afternoon.[16] Sam coveted that monkey. When he asked for it, his father told him it was to be a present for Sam's mother, but that he would carve another for Sam some day. The father forgot the promise and the son did, too—until his father was about to die. Then he reminded his father of that broken promise. Shortly thereafter Sam received a package in the mail. Although that long-delayed peachseed monkey had broken in the carver's hands, so that it came glued together, it became, in Keen's retelling, a monkey of parabolic power—the power to unlock the meaning of Keen's own life and his understanding of his father's and the power to throw new light on his understanding of the God of promise of whom the biblical narratives speak.

Yet another quality informs the telling of life stories when they are well told, as the examples cited readily indicate. Memory has

140

vested these events with vivid, specific, colorful detail, and thus conveyed them incarnate to our imaginations. They are stories we can recognize in their real-life settings, events like those which have happened to us. When Augustine hears the voices of children playing in the garden next door, we hear them, too. When Steffens sits alone on the front steps waiting, we can feel that hard surface through the seat of our pants, too. With Gandhi we face the difficulty of having our hostess serve us delicacies we detest, of trying not to taste the oysters or the curry or the liver or whatever we must force ourselves to eat.

One final feature of lively autobiography deserves mention. In almost every case I can think of, surely in every case mentioned, the past events profoundly shaping present lives are interpersonal events. Often they are intergenerational stories—stories about Augustine and his mother, stories about Sam Keen and his father. At other times they tell us only about casual encounters, such as that of Gandhi and his British hosts. But in both cases, because they are personal, they are to a very important degree open-ended. How we interpret them, how we incorporate them into our ongoing life histories counts more heavily than any clear-cut moral inherent in the event itself.

Learning to *tell* one's personal history in a style reflecting the qualities we have been thinking of is a mode of self-transcendence which complements retelling the story of God's people as a whole through the ages, and telling the tale of our times in its many-colored fullness and variety. Learning to *listen* to the stories of our own lives and of the lives of all our sisters and brothers, grandfathers and grandmothers helps us to listen to and learn from our whole past, including our past in Palestine in the days of Rahab and of Jesus. We need to claim our roots in "history" and to stretch ourselves with the aid of that elastic concept.

All three strata of our history that we have been considering in this chapter call us out of bondage to the here and the now. All three ask us to interpret the past in order to decide who we want to be today. All three ask us to exercise our freedom to choose where we have come from and where we are going. Where we are going and who we are becoming is the subject of our next chapter. The story we tell about ourselves today is not the same one we will have to tell tomorrow. We can begin now with "Once upon a time." We cannot yet end with a flourishing "And they all lived happily ever after." Our stories must therefore remain like the installments in a serial, with a certain cliffhanging quality to them. For as self-transcendent human beings, we are open to the future as well as to the past. That adventure lies before us.

NOTES

1. As quoted by John Black, *The Dominion of Man* (Edinburgh: Edinburgh University Press, 1970), p. 10.

2. Wolfhart Pannenberg, *What is Man?: Contemporary Anthropology in Theological Perspective* (Philadelphia: Fortress Press, 1970), p. 138.

3. Carl Becker, "What Are Historical Facts?", as quoted by Van Austin Harvey, *The Historian and the Believer* (Philadelphia: Westminster Press, 1966, 1981), p. 204.

4. Carl Becker, "Detachment and the Writing of History," as quoted by Alan Richardson, *History Sacred and Profane* (Philadelphia: Westminster Press, 1964), p. 173.

5. W. Taylor Stevenson, *History as Myth* (New York: Seabury Press, 1969), p. 15.

6. James B. Wiggins, "The Release of History Through Myth," *Anglican Theological Review* 59 (1977): 157.

7. Harvey, *Historian*, p. 78.

8. Pauli Murray, *Proud Shoes: The Story of an American Family* (New York: Harper & Row, 1978).

9. Julia O'Faolain and Lauro Martines, eds., *Not in God's Image* (New York: Harper & Row, 1973).

10. Elise Boulding, *The Underside of History: A View of Women Through Time* (Boulder, Colorado: Westview Press, 1976).

11. Elizabeth Cady Stanton, *The Woman's Bible* (1895–98, facsimile ed., Seattle, Wash.: Coalition Task Force on Women and Religion, 1974).

12. Quoted from "Press Comments", ibid., following Part I, p. 152.

13. Gerda Lerner, *The Female Experience* (Indianapolis: The Bobbs-Merrill Co., 1977).

14. Adrienne Rich, Review of *The Female Experience* in *New York Times Book Review* (March 20, 1977), p. 11.

15. Robert and Jane Hallowell Coles, *Women of Crisis* (New York: Delacorte Press/Seymour Lawrence: 1978, 1980).

16. Sam Keen, *To a Dancing God* (New York: Harper & Row, 1970), pp. 100–101.

CHAPTER ELEVEN

Creating the Future

Jesus said, "No one who puts his hand to the plow and looks back is fit for the kingdom of God" (Luke 9:62). The forward thrust of such a saying pulls us around sharply. No nostalgia for a golden past is permitted those made in the image of God. Not only are we rooted in the past; we are also summoned into the future.

Conscious movement toward the not-yet is one more distinctively human activity separating us (as far as we know) from the rest of the animal world. We human beings are able to think about the year 2084. Thoughtful men and women today have radically differing ideas, however, of what that year holds for our successors, if any, on the planet. A look at those differences will aid reflection about human ability to use the future tense. *

The spectrum runs from great optimism about tomorrow to stark pessimism. Since there are so many so-called futurists now breaking into print, it would be easy to find dozens of popular views on either end. In 1980 one astute editor headlined the review of a new book on the dark end "Future Fluff." Another had the wit to head a column: "Long-Range Forecast: Sunny for the Next Millennium." In the latter case, the caption highlighted a forecast that by the year 2175 the per capita income worldwide will have risen to $20,000 in 1979 dollars, and the global population will have leveled off at 10 billion.

143

* Herein lie both blessing and curse: we may hope or be anxious?

Serious and sobering voices speak darkly about the future, too—voices which don't often capture the headlines in weekly magazines. One of them deserves special attention from Christians—that of Richard L. Rubenstein. Rubenstein asks us to question deeply whether there is any hope for the human race. He does not think that we can believe any longer in a guaranteed future.

The grim reality of Auschwitz haunts all of Rubenstein's thinking about human being. He is convinced that after Auschwitz no one can continue to believe in a just God active in history. While he was still a student at Hebrew Union College, he read in a newspaper one day about the "huge piles of ownerless shoes" at that Nazi death camp in Poland. It was his first realization of what was being done to his fellow human beings, by other human beings, that day, even as he was getting ready to go to his "field placement" job as a student rabbi.

His vision of those ownerless shoes changed Rubenstein's thinking. Never afterwards was he content with either the rationalism or the optimism of Reform Judaism, or with its belief that education would eventually end anti-Semitism. "The revelation of the death camps," he recalls, "caused me to reject the whole optimistic theology of liberal religion."[1] Since then his writings are marked by his conviction that there are no innocent persons, that we are and always will be a problem to ourselves because of our deep-seated desire to get rid of God.

As Rubenstein understands our present cultural situation, we are already living in *the last days*. No intelligent human being can any longer hope for the coming of the kingdom, he thinks, in either a biblical or a Marxist sense. And this is not simply because, given our new capability for "instantaneous megamurder," every day is potentially the last day for the human race. It is equally because of a shift in our time-sense. We are no longer able to perceive time as our biblical ancestors did. Electronic technology and the collapse of religious belief in life after death have together altered our sequential experience in time, Rubenstein argues. Linear time no longer has decisive meaning for us.

Individually, we are in the position of Mersault at the end of Camus's novel *The Stranger*, "totally incapable of being future-oriented." "When we confront the undeceived sensibility of contem-
144

porary man without evasion," Rubenstein claims, "we find ourselves face to face with Mersault."[2] He knows only today. *Now* has
become the critical time, because tomorrow may be too late.

Corporately, we are experiencing a return to the cyclical time-
view of archaic, preliterate people, he thinks. We understand that
the survival of the species depends just on the unending repetition
of the birth-death cycle of its individual members. If we are realists
without any apocalyptic illusions, we accept the fact: "There is no
coming kingdom."[3]

A quite different reading of our sense of time informs the writings of many other theologians in our generation. They do not
subscribe either to the thesis that truly modern men and women
can no longer be oriented toward the future, nor to the thesis that
only Nothingness lies ahead. Human beings cannot be human
without the horizon of the future, these theologians say.

At first, the phrase "the horizon of the future" seems almost a
contradiction in terms. We commonly think of the horizon as if it
were the boundary line between earth and heaven, the sort of
horizontal line a child draws so firmly on a crayoned landscape. It
seems to us to be a spatial rather than a temporal concept. But on
second thought, the image gains power and dynamism. As any
hiker or sailor knows, the horizon is always ahead of you—a moving, changing summons to go forward.

A dynamic sense of time which includes a changed and changing
future is surely one of the hallmarks of the modern consciousness.
Thanks to technology we have a new and sometimes frightening
sense of acceleration in the rate of change. Our grandparents
walked to school, they told us. We took the schoolbus. To get their
education our great-grandchildren may just sit home in the "media
room," as the old den is now being called, and push the buttons
on the console.

Over and above a response evoked by the rapid pace of change
in our environment, however, three *intellectual currents* have contributed to our altered theological sense of tomorrow. The *first* is
the revolution in the physical and biological sciences. Unstable at-
oms and evolving species dissolve static reality. The universe is
charged with motion. The *second* is philosophical reflection on the
nature of time, especially that of Ernst Bloch, who greatly stimu-

lated Christian thinking about "the consciousness which runs ahead."[4] Bloch, in fact, suggested that the future has ontological priority over the present, an idea so unfamiliar that it threatens us, as Carl Braaten put it memorably, with a "hernia of the mind."[5] The *third* is the recovery in our time of a renewed understanding of biblical eschatology.

Before we elaborate that third intellectual development, however, one further comment is necessary about the altered time-sense which causes theologians to stress the impact of the future on human selfhood. The phrase "linear time," as used by Rubenstein and many others to draw a contrast between Hebraic thought and the cyclical thought of other ancient people, fails to do justice to the new sensibility we are discussing. The term "linear," to describe the sequence of past-present-future, too easily suggests the monotony of parallel railroad tracks running straight across Texas into a vanishing point. Or again, it suggests the kind of hypnotic fixation on the straight line which Marshall McLuhan blamed on Gutenberg and dubbed "newspaper somnambulism."

The language being used in Christian anthropology to discuss our openness to the future is decisively not the language of a line of cold type. Jürgen Moltmann, for example, links the concept of the future both to the fact of human freedom and to a "rich quantity of unrealized possibilities" latent in the present. Every present in history, he says in his work on *Man,* is "pregnant with its future."[6] If one takes such language seriously, the future yet to be born is not already fed into a computer program.

Not surprisingly, Wolfhart Pannenberg also uses metaphors of birth when talking in *What is Man?* about orientation to the future. He believes that it is not natural for us to live only for today, and that even when we try to do so, we cannot suppress questions about the future. We plan for it. We always try to conceive and to create a more satisfactory world. But, he insists,

> It is possible to calculate the future in terms of the present only to a very small degree, even though human science has made great strides in that direction. The essential nature of the future lies in the unpredictable new thing that is hidden in the womb of the future. This often enough thwarts all human plans. . . . [7]

What is essentially human about our relation to the future, Pan-

146

nenberg continues in a happy turn of phrase, is "the venturesome impetus into the open."[8]

Both Moltmann and Pannenberg are among the contemporary theologians who have been collectively described as teachers in the Theology of Hope school. Such a label fails to recognize the distinctiveness of each man's thought. Nevertheless, they both give the idea of human hope a major place in their anthropology and, along with their colleagues in the school, help us therefore to think further about the future, and specifically about the recovery of biblical eschatology which has put its mark on today's ideas about tomorrow.

Two themes are of utmost importance to all the theologians of hope, and they are themes which give content to Christian self-understanding about the future—the themes of *the kingdom of God* and of *the resurrection of Jesus Christ*. Rubenstein, as we noted earlier, said that no one can believe any longer in the coming of the kingdom. These thinkers do. Rubenstein also said (and in this instance, too, was a spokesman for thousands of intellectuals) that no one believes any longer in life after death. These thinkers do. But, they all express their convictions in a manner far different from the liberal theological optimism which Rubenstein rejected after Auschwitz.

New Testament scholarship in this century agrees unanimously that the kingdom of God was at the heart of Jesus' teaching and preaching. It takes seriously the apocalyptic imagery in the gospels. It rejects the notion that when Jesus proclaimed the good news, "The kingdom of God is at hand," he was talking about warm and cozy feelings in individual hearts. Rather, he was talking about the in-breaking of God's future into the present. In making God's kingdom the central motif of his message, Jesus awakened lively and eager anticipation. The common people gladly heard him.

However much the gospel of the kingdom is a welcome and essential basis of Christian hope in the present, it is a part of Christian tradition which poses problems for self-understanding today. Many people find it difficult to enter into the symbolism of monarchy. Language about the rule and reign of the Almighty God has little power over the imagination of Democrats or Republicans, much less Communists. Kingdom talk, in fact, is often heard as an alienating blah.

147

Conscious of this problem, one theologian of hope proposed that we should abandon the ancient symbol and translate its significance by simply using the phrase, "the power of the future."[9] It is difficult to settle for such a solution. What would it feel like to pray daily, "Our Father, let the power of your future come. . . . "? The abstraction ignores the power of concrete metaphor to energize the religious imagination.

A more serious problem related to the kingdom of God is deliberately raised by the title of this chapter, which claims that human beings are participants in creating the future. How can that claim be reconciled with the unequivocal consensus of mainstream Christian theology that *we* do not create God's kingdom, God does?

The history of Christian thought could be written around answers to that question and all the subsidiary questions about grace and freedom, sin and redemption, time and eternity which come with it. The extreme poles appear and reappear through the centuries, together with various median positions. On the one hand some Christians believed and believe that times are bad and that they are going to get worse. All we can do is put on our white robes, climb a tree, and wait for the second coming. God himself will usher in his kingdom with a flourish of trumpets. On the other hand, other Christians believed and believe that we must roll up our sleeves, grab hammer and saw, ballot and petition, and go about the business of building God's kingdom here on earth.

Those are caricatures of theological extremes, of course, but they help mark out the territory. If we remember at this point that we are trying to focus on openness to the future as ingredient in becoming human, I think we can blaze a trail through that territory. First, we need to insist that the kingdom of God, the rule, the reign, the sovereignty of God, is already a reality. It is not something that you or I or all of humanity together must set forth to bring into being. Second, we need to affirm that the human consequences of God's sovereignty were made explicit in the life of Jesus of Nazareth. He lived, to use that idiom, "already" in God's kingdom. Third, we who are being conformed to his image may help create our common future as he did—by walking in the way of the cross. Once again, Christology informs anthropology.

Among so-called theologians of hope, Moltmann has done as

much as anyone to make that clear. In his treatment of Christian anthropology he divides the polar choices I have just caricatured into the comparable categories of "inward emigration" and "Utopian consciousness." It is noteworthy that he judges the former attitude far more harshly than the latter. "If there is any attitude of criticism towards culture to which Christians have tied themselves very closely in the recent past," he writes, "it is this inward emigration into the private, the esoteric, and the nonpolitical. But should not authentic Christian belief prepare rather for the incarnation of the human in inhuman circumstances, even if this means denying oneself and taking up one's cross?"[10] When he begins to speak of Utopian consciousness, on the other hand, he is quick to say, "I do not mean anything negative by this."[11]

Nevertheless, when he comes to discussion of life lived in hope, in the closing paragraphs of his book, Utopian thought is remodeled in the form of the cross. Hope, Moltmann believes, alters us because it shows us new possibilities. It makes us come out of ourselves to walk in love. This is so because Christian hope is grounded in the memory of Jesus Christ and him crucified. Therefore it sees the human future not in terms of our progress, but in terms of sacrifice. The Christian Utopia is bound to the future of the Son of man who found no place to lay his head. It lies with all the others who have no place in the world. "The Christian hope, in so far as it is Christian, is the hope of those who have no future. It is therefore a hope in contradiction of self-satisfied optimists and of equally self-satisfied pessimists."[12]

Christian hope for the future not only makes the kingdom of God its content, a kingdom defined by the love of the crucified God, but also makes Easter central in its thought about the future. Jesus' resurrection from the dead does not just offer us pious and pietistic hope for individual survival after clinical death. It was an event whereby Jesus became, to borrow Braaten's words again, "the fulcrum of the future." His successful love is a proleptic embodiment of the final future of humankind. The forgiveness offered through the risen Lord is an eschatological gift of grace. The God who raised Jesus from death to life is the God of our tomorrow.

Our role in creating the future is therefore a responsive one, as we have frequently had occasion to insist; but it is equally a responsible one. We are not called to be passive. We are called to expectancy. Expectancy, as I understand it, is best captured in the shining eyes of a child on Christmas Eve. Keen anticipation of the morning keeps such a child awake. She is genuinely open to the future.

Reflection on being human as being full of hope leads to a corollary emphasis on being shaped by the questions one asks. What we have been talking about includes the recognition that our human capacity for self-transcendence, and therefore for hope, is closely related to our ability to ask questions. Through our anticipations and our hopes, we inquire beyond ourselves, beyond the horizon of our present. We "strike out into the realm of the unknown, beyond every answer that has already been reached."[13]

We climb a mountain because we expect to reach the top. We ask questions because we think that an answer is possible. Although we ourselves are at the heart of the questions we pose, we reach out into the world and beyond in search of clues to solve the mystery of our own being. In the very process of questioning, we are driven into an open future. Yet we are already existentially involved with the answer we seek. And, in Christian perspective, the most radical modern questioning about ultimate reality cannot outstrip the biblical God toward whose future we are moving.

Each of us is by definition an "inquiring who." That is one of the reasons why human transformation is possible. Along with Pannenberg and Braaten, Michael Novak is one of the contemporary theologians who has helpfully affirmed this human gift as a gift which enables us to change the world. Question-asking, Novak argues, is fundamental in all intelligent social and political action, as well as in all metaphysical and theological reflection. Our ability to ask ever new questions makes it possible to move forward. Responsible work toward the community of love and justice proclaimed in the gospel of Jesus Christ depends at every step, he thinks, "upon the relentlessness and the skills of the drive to ask questions."[14]

As we cultivate the art of asking questions, as we continue to question "who we are, under these stars, and with the wind upon our faces," we need, in Novak's terms, "tutored subjectivity."[15] We need to know what others have learned on their voyages of dis-

150

covery, their ascents of the mountain. Human questions and human answers from the past can spark fresh questions in our minds. But no pre-packaged answers from the past can serve as final answers to questions about ourselves or about the future which is God's future.

Our everyday vocabularies of tomorrow contain the words and the ideas we have developed in this chapter: forecast, promise, hope, expectancy. Whether we consider ourselves to be optimists, pessimists, or that balance of the two which allows us smugly to call ourselves realists, we listen to forecasts and make our own. Even when it is only a question of tomorrow's weather (and whether we prefer to predict that it will be partly sunny or partly cloudy), we project ourselves into the future. In celebrating this special human trait, Christian anthropology claims that men and women are related to a God who makes and keeps promises about our future. That God has created us with a built-in freedom to change and be changed. Christian hope carries with it the lively expectation that the God who makes all things new will transform the whole creation, human society—and you and me. In the final chapter we will ask questions about that transformation.

NOTES

1. Richard L. Rubenstein, *After Auschwitz: Radical Theology and Contemporary Judaism* (Indianapolis: Bobbs-Merrill Co., 1966), p. 216.

2. Richard L. Rubenstein, *Morality and Eros* (New York: McGraw-Hill Book Co., 1970), p. 13.

3. Ibid., p. 15.

4. Jürgen Moltmann, *Man: Christian Anthropology in the Conflicts of the Present* (Philadelphia: Fortress Press, 1974), p. 42.

5. Carl E. Braaten and Robert W. Jenson, *The Futurist Option* (Westminster, Md.: Newman Press, 1970), p. 28.

6. Moltman, *Man*, p. 42.

7. Wolfhart Pannenberg, *What is Man?: Contemporary Anthropology in Theological Perspective* (Philadelphia: Fortress Press, 1972), p. 42.

8. Ibid., p. 51.

9. Braaten and Jenson, *The Futurist Option*, p. 84.

10. Moltmann, *Man*, p. 41.

11. Ibid., p. 42.

12. Ibid., p. 117.

13. Braaten and Jenson, *The Futurist Option*, p. 22.

14. Michael Novak, "The Absolute Future," *New Theology No. 5*, ed. Martin E. Marty and Dean G. Peerman (New York: Macmillan Publishing Co., 1968), p. 209.

15. Michael Novak, *Ascent of the Mountain, Flight of the Dove* (New York: Harper & Row, 1971), p. 208.

CHAPTER TWELVE

Being
Transformed

Homo sapiens does not inherit a fixed and unchanging human nature. We are flexible animals with a rich repertoire of gifts and powers. Along with the gifts and powers of relationship already examined in these pages, one more calls for our wondering attention. We are able to worship. And thereby we are able to be transformed.

Human transformation is not normally accomplished overnight. It is not normally an event which can be tagged with date and time of day, as some "twice-born" Christians would lead us to believe. Instead, it is one of the long processes of becoming. St. Francis knew that well. After twenty years as a full-time Christian, he said to his followers, "Let us begin . . . to serve our Lord God, for until now we have made but little progress." But in this department, "progress" is very difficult to measure. Taking one's own spiritual pulse is probably a symptom of illness. To change the metaphor, continually pulling oneself up by the roots to see how well one is growing is likely to be as damaging to human spiritual development as it would be to a zinnia plant.

Nevertheless, the process of such growth and transformation has been documented by a noble army of people whose lives and writings witness to this possibility. Their experience and their testimony can well help us to consider this final mode of self-transcend-

153

ence. As we think about transformation with the help of these witnesses, we will discover anew that human life is both irreducibly social and irreducibly singular. No one establishes a living relationship with God alone; no one is ever transformed in isolation from other human beings. Even a devout hermit in his cell on Mount Athos prays in the fellowship of the Body of Christ. Even well-trained choristers singing God's praises in unison contribute distinctive voices. If I go into my own room and shut the door to pray, I remain a part of the communion of saints. Yet in my most deeply corporate experience of worship, I also remain an individual and become even more myself through that experience.

A long-established Christian idiom underlines the reality that we move toward maturity on two parallel tracks. We speak normally of "prayer and worship." In common understanding "prayer" usually refers to what we do alone and "worship" to what we do together. The distinction is misleading in many ways, but it is helpful if we insist that the idiom wear hyphens: prayer-and-worship. Prayer-and-worship is a unified human activity leading us on the path of growth and transformation.

St. Paul is one of many Christian saints who walked that path. He is one of the earliest witnesses to the possibility of human transformation. Reliable information about his life is tantalizingly limited. In spite of the numerous full-length biographies and studies of Paul of Tarsus we know very little about his experience from his own mouth, that is, from his epistles. When we add what we know from St. Luke's account in *Acts* we find that the two accounts are not entirely in agreement. For example, St. Luke dramatizes Paul's blindness in the Damascus Road episode, whereas Paul himself insists that he *saw* the Lord. All of the evidence, however, shows that this giant sculptor of Christian tradition was not transformed in a sudden once-for-all metamorphosis. He unquestionably grew in wisdom and in stature through his relationship with the living Lord.

Luke's terse remark that the young man named Saul was a front-row onlooker at the stoning of Stephen strongly suggests that there was psychic preparation for the conversion en route to Damascus. Paul's own report of a later visit with St. Peter for more than two weeks in Jerusalem strongly suggests a subsequent process of learning through asking questions. Whatever the difficulties of es-

154 *Paul needed instruction in the Christian faith from other persons.

tablishing the chronology of Paul's extant letters and of proving a development of his thought on that basis, he certainly changed his mind on some subjects. And he insisted that other Christians should anticipate being changed. He exhorts them to seek it.

Three Pauline quotations give us the texture of his thought on this subject of change. I shall use the paraphrastic translation of the New English Bible because it helps us to hear old familiar words afresh.

First, "we shall all be changed" (1 Cor. 15:51). In Paul's opinion that is a straightforward statement of fact. Paul, using the future tense, is trying to tell the Christians in Corinth what to expect, what he understands about resurrection. It is not mere continuity of life beyond the grave, not mere immortality. It is something new. It is a condition completely different from what they have experienced walking about the streets of Corinth. By this very matter-of-fact attitude he invites his readers to open themselves to future transformation.

Second, and of major importance for our theme, "Adapt yourselves no longer to the pattern of this present world, but let your minds be remade and your whole nature thus transformed" (Rom. 12:2). In the King James Version the imperative rings more clearly, "Be ye transformed. . . . " But in both translations what Paul thinks is patently clear: transformation is possible, indeed inevitable, if one engages in worship with one's total being, not just with a portion of oneself. This transformation represents not just a change of mental outlook, although the intellect is certainly included. Rather, it is so thorough-going as to force him to say:

> I implore you by God's mercy to offer your very selves to him: a living sacrifice, dedicated and fit for his acceptance, the worship offered by mind and heart.
>
> (Rom. 12:1)

For St. Paul, life in relation to Jesus Christ, life *in* Christ as he called it, is one which increasingly bears fruit.

The opening paragraph in his letter to the Christians at Philippi provides the third example of his thought on the process of transformation. He expects them to continue to grow, and he is convinced that such growth is the Lord's doing, not merely the result of strenuous spiritual calisthenics on their part. He joyfully remembers them in his prayers, Paul tells the Philippian Christians;

Paul is also pastoral at times and gives different emphases to ideas to one church or another

155

he appears to have been especially fond of them. But then he adds, "Of one thing I am certain: the One who started the good work in you will bring it to completion by the Day of Christ Jesus" (NEB Phil. 1:6). On the strength of that certainty, he tells these friends further that he is praying that their love may grow "ever richer and richer. . . . " (Phil. 1:9).

Paul did not do all of his praying off by himself. As we would put it today, he also "went to church." His instructions on how to conduct corporate worship decently and in order, his frequent quotation of hymns and liturgical phrases used in worship, the communal nature of almost all his extant correspondence—all show us a man who himself grew through coming together with other Christians on the first day of the week to praise God and listen to his voice. It is noteworthy that he delivered to the church at Corinth the traditions for celebrating the Eucharist in virtually the same words he used about delivering to them the good news of the gospel "as of first importance" (Cf. 1 Cor. 11:23–26 and 15:3–11).

St. Augustine is another great spokesman for the transforming power of prayer and worship. He speaks simply and naturally about it. His *Confessions* are begun, continued, and ended in prayer. They were written after Augustine had been a Christian for fifteen years. They show what those fifteen years of "living the Faith" had done to him, as one modern translator observed. If we go back and reread some of Augustine's earlier works, they seem thin and pallid after the "full-bloodedness" of the *Confessions*.[1] That comment points to the process of transformation occuring in the personal life of the Bishop of Hippo. It also echoes the Pauline idea that prayer and worship are full-time activities of the whole person—not of something called just the soul or the spirit, nor of a person just when he or she is being "religious."

Three of Augustine's own prayers further illustrate that intimacy with God which had now become the reality in which he consciously moved and had his being. Speaking to God about his earlier life, he acknowledged, "You were there before me, but I had gone away from myself, and I could not find even myself, much less You." His new environment, or rather his new awareness of the true environment, provided a way of self-discovery. He was able to know who he was.

His new self-knowledge led in turn to an urge to ascribe to God all the vitality and all the love he experienced:

> Be You our glory. Let us be loved for Your sake and let Your word be praised in us. For when You are our strength it is strength indeed, when it is our own it is all weakness.

And he understood fully that this strong and lively power was a gift given through Jesus Christ:

> If I had not sought the way to You in Christ our Savior, I would have come not to instruction but to destruction. See, Lord, I cast my care upon You, that I may live.

Augustine's life of prayer, his personal journey toward human wholeness, was no more solitary than St. Paul's. In fact, when one reads about the intensely busy and intensely public life he lived as Bishop of Hippo, one marvels that he found time to be alone for prayer. He spent what would seem to us an inordinate amount of time in church. One biographer notes that he not only participated in a daily Eucharist, which he referred to as the "daily physic of the body of the Lord"[2] but that he also preached as many as four times a week. Since some of Augustine's sermons lasted as long as two or three hours, one has a great deal of sympathy for the faithful Christians standing crowded together in the nave while their celebrated bishop sat in his chair, his *cathedra,* expounding the Psalms or St John's gospel for them.

Speaking of baptism in one of his writings, Augustine comments directly on the process of growth and change we are now considering. The baptized person is truly "renovated" in that holy bath, he says, and becomes "steadily better from day to day, though with some progress is quicker than with others. For one sees, if one watches carefully and without prejudice, that many really do make progress in this new life."[3] He drives home his point by quoting the Apostle Paul, "Though our outer nature is wasting away, our inner nature is being renewed every day" (2 Cor. 4:16).

Although Augustine was thoroughly a man of prayer—the *Confessions* have the tone of an extended conversation with his Lord— he reports that like most of us he experienced the difficulty of keeping his mind on his prayers. "The great business of praying," he wrote, "is broken off through the onrush of every idle thought." This phenomenon of distraction in prayer, as it is classically called,

Prayer should be both dialogical and theological. 157

is known to all the saints. A nineteenth-century spiritual director, Theophan the Recluse, offered some sage advice on the subject: "Make yourself a rule always to be with the Lord, keeping your mind in your heart and do not let your thoughts wander; as often as they stray, turn them back again and keep them at home in the closet of your heart. . . ."[4] He seems to be saying that the mind can monitor the heart in converse with the Lord. The injunction to keep one's mind in the heart is strikingly similar to Paul's injunction to be transformed by the renewal of the mind. We do not need to check our intellects at the door when we enter the halls of worship.

We need to stress again that we are thinking about the transformation of the whole human being, not just some portion of the self. Today's renewed interest in Christian "spirituality" is making an important contribution to Christian self-understanding, but the term "spirituality" all too easily suggests that we are disembodied spirits and not concerned about the whole person in relation to God. It needs to be clear also that "spirituality" is not an esoteric discipline for a special few who have special gifts for sanctity. Men and women of our own century who knew themselves called to be saints can help us think about those dimensions of wholeness and normality, perhaps even more effectively than figures like Augustine and Paul whom we are likely to think of wearing halos.

Evelyn Underhill comes to mind first, not only because she was a renowned scholar in the field of worship in the first half of this century, but also because she exhibited in her own personhood the fruits of that transformation about which she often spoke and wrote. Recalling his first meeting with her, one friend said that when she rose from her chair and came to greet him, he was almost thrown off balance by the radiance of her face. Light simply streamed from it. He added, "It told one not only of *herself*, but more of God and of the Mystical Body than all her work put together."[5] One is reminded of Moses' shining countenance when he came down from the mountain after talking with Yahweh. Evidently, Underhill was a woman who spoke from experience.

When she talks about worship, Underhill talks explicitly about human transformation. Speaking once to a Fellowship of Prayer in the Church of Scotland, for example, she said, "You are, or should be, agents or transmitters of the transforming, redeeming

158

power of God."[6] Her meditations sometimes sound out of date today. But if one can avoid being put off, for example, by what Marconi lately said about the discovery of the wireless, one encounters great practical wisdom. No one that I know of was more consistently social in her interpretation of prayer.

"A real man or woman of prayer," she said, "should be a live wire, a link between God's grace and the world that needs it."[7] She understood worship as "the great spiritual action" of the human race, an action in which we transcend our ordinary visible world and join with the whole communion of saints to delight in God. She recognized that we worship corporately even when we worship alone in the privacy of our own rooms. She affirmed that we are incarnate beings, not pure spirits, so that music and symbolism and sacraments and what we do with our hands and feet play a rightful part in our corporate turning to God.

At the end of a lecture given in 1929 Underhill quoted from the Anglican liturgy: "Here we offer and present unto thee, O Lord, ourselves, our souls and bodies. . . . " God asks not for our gifts, but for ourselves, she commented. And then, "Worship is the response of humanity to that wonderful demand."[8]

Such consistent emphasis on worship as humanity's corporate action needs, however, as a necessary complement, the insight that we also need to pray alone. Jesus went to the synagogue, "as his custom was." He also went out alone into the hills to pray. In a brief but durable book on prayer and worship, the modern Quaker, *Douglas Steere,* made solitude the first condition of prayer. Although he recognized as fully as Underhill the need for regular public worship, Steere also knew that what happens when we gather together for worship is enriched and deepened by the quality of life each person brings to such a meeting. He therefore urged Christians to carve out time and space for private prayer.

A commonsense, practical man, Steere recognized that it is difficult for busy men and women to find such time and space, especially if there are several small children in the household. Yet he also recognized that we can always find time for what we think is important. Even as St. Francis escaped from his brothers so that he could be made fit to be among them, so we too must seek out privacy. Prayer in such solitude, Steere believed, is simply a "form of waking up out of the dull sleep in which our life has been spent."

159

Even more graphically, prayer is a "dip into acid."[9] It is where we discover the center of validity.

What should people do when they go apart to encounter that center? The modern French writer *Simone Weil* summed up a whole library of spiritual instruction on that subject in one word: wait. Her own experience of waiting on God was a tormented one. She knew much about that dark night of the soul of which the mystics write. She identified deeply with the poor and the suffering—working in factories, practicing voluntary poverty, always trying consciously to live, as she put it, "at the intersection of Christianity and everything that is not Christianity."[10] She once observed, "Waiting patiently in expectation is the foundation of the spiritual life."[11]

Yet that waiting, that patience, that expectancy bore fruit in Weil's life. She knew moments of intense awareness of God's presence, moments when she was surprised by joy. One of those times occurred when she was reciting the George Herbert poem "Love," which begins, "Love bade me welcome. . . . " "I used to think I was merely reciting it as a beautiful poem," she recalled, "but without my knowing it, the recitation had the virtue of a prayer. It was during one of these recitations that Christ himself came down and took possession of me."[12]

Without her knowing it, the poem had become prayer, had become the vehicle of Christ's reaching out and claiming her. That dimension of the process of human transformation—God is doing something for us and through us whether we know it or not—undergirds the whole theology of Christian personhood, as well as that portion of it which reflects about our own capacities for prayer. God calls for our whole lives in corporate worship and in the stillness at the center of our solitude. He calls us to wait for him with a lively expectancy. But in all the time of waiting, God's love is at work. As Weil said of people in darkness, "God himself sets their faces in the right direction."[13]

We have come to the heart of what must rightly be called the paradox of prayer. It calls for steady effort on our part, but at the same time it is given as a gift. Writing about this paradox, *Henri Nouwen* underlines its seeming contradiction. "We cannot plan, organize or manipulate God," he reminds us, "but without a careful discipline, we cannot receive him either."[14] This is undoubtedly a paradox in the sense of being different from our ordinary opinions, a paradox similar to that of the familiar phrase, "in whose service is perfect freedom." But it rests on the logic of relationships.

We cannot capture anyone else's love in a net woven of our own strivings. But we can and must reach out to the other, consistently, patiently, thoughtfully. In the last analysis, the response of love is always a gift freely given.

Each one of us is called by God to an adventure of human transformation through prayer-and-worship. In the process we enter into the great public work of Christian worship, a liturgy in which we participate with all our brothers and sisters in Christ from St. Paul's day to our own. In the process we also enter into those disciplines of prayer that help us grow in discipleship. There are many ways to pray. One of Henri Nouwen's contributions to contemporary discussion of Christian spirituality is his sane emphasis that each of us needs to discover our own way to pray. He gives us fresh permission to create our own recipe for a living relationship with God at the same time that he insists we can do nothing without God's initiative.

"Just as artists search for the style that is more their own so people who pray search for the prayer of their heart," Nouwen writes.[15] Since there are many spiritualities, many ways to God, which one has my name on it? Once one has discovered that prayer is the best way to strip off illusions and adopt "the basic receptive attitude out of which all life can receive new vitality," he or she will raise that question. The answer is to try them and find out.

So far in this chapter we have been thinking about the balance between the communal and the individual in the process of human transformation—both in the lives and thought of two great saints of the early church and in the lives and thought of four modern men and women on the way to sanctification. In conclusion I want to suggest one more way of walking along that transforming path. *We can walk in partnership.*

Human liberation and human transformation are two names for the same phenomenon. Throughout this study I have recurrently spoken of human being created in the image of God, male and female. As one reads about our shared past in the church of Christ, one of the surprises in the pages of history is the amazing degree

161

to which men and women transcended their own times and their own stereotypes when they were engaged together in the adventure of a life of prayer.

Our earthbound vocabularies have trouble naming this fact from our past. Most of the literature uses the anemic term "spiritual friendship" to describe this relationship of mutual growth. Two partnerships from our history, chosen from a wide range of possibilities, will show both the limitations of that phrase and its pertinence. The examples come from the departments of Christian tradition which the textbooks label respectively "monasticism" and "mysticism."

The first two friends are *St. Clare* and *St. Francis*. Both lived in the Italian hill town of Assisi. Francis and his small group of brothers were together in the chapel of Portiuncula. Late one night Clare, then seventeen, slipped away from home and joined them. Her hair was shorn and she was given Francis's own habit to wear. Thus in the spring of 1212 began the "second order" of Franciscans.

Biographers seem unable to write about the event without discomfort. One called it "an incident which we can hardly record with satisfaction." With far greater perception, although in equally stilted language, G. K. Chesterton commented, "As soon as we assume for a moment as a hypothesis what St. Francis and St. Clare assumed all the time as an absolute, that there is a direct divine relation more glorious than any romance, the story of St. Clare's elopement is simply a romance with a happy ending."[16]

The best assessment of the event that I have read occurs in Laurence Housman's play about Sister Clare. At the end of a very amusing scene in which Brother Juniper fights off Temptation in the person of Clare, Francis answers the question why Clare has come. The answer is very simple: "God sent her. . . . If we have brothers, must we not have sisters as well?" And to the further question, "But what can she do, Father?" comes the reply, "Bring others; work as we do; give service; love poverty; find freedom; have joy!"[17]

In Spain, over two hundred years later, another woman and another man shared a partnership in the faith of equal importance for their future and ours. We know them from history as *St. Teresa of Avila* and *St. John of the Cross*. In this case Teresa was the mentor and John the beneficiary of her prior experience with the Lord. It can be argued convincingly that the spirituality of the medieval church was shaped by men and women *together* far more than is the case today.

Teresa, although she has sometimes been dismissed as the patron saint of hysterics, was actually a vigorous, witty, and intelligent woman. She reformed the Carmelite order, founded new convents, and wrote with authority about the spiritual life. Perhaps her best known work is *The Interior Castle,* a description of "the progress" of the soul. In the language of that day, one can move through seven mansions—from humility through prayer and discipline and quest to spiritual betrothal and then, after a period of increased temptation, to spiritual marriage. In the epilogue of her work, completed in 1577, Teresa reminded her sisters that, while they might enjoy themselves in this Interior Castle, they could not enter all of the mansions on their own power. The Lord of the Castle must admit them.

Teresa's greatest disciple, St. John of the Cross, was equally aware of the fact that God the Holy Spirit directs our journeys toward fulfillment. Following Teresa, he also borrowed the erotic imagery of the "Song of Songs" to talk about the estate of spiritual marriage, the union of love with God. His *Spiritual Canticle* remains a classic on "the progress of the loving soul." It is noteworthy that St. John, who finished this masterpiece of devotional literature in 1584, seven years after Teresa had finished her most noted work, praises in its pages just two sources—Holy Scripture and the writings of his friend Teresa.[18]

Francis and Clare, Teresa and John were not disembodied spirits. They were full-blooded human beings launched on the adventure of transformation by the power and activity of God. Yet they come before us as symbolic figures, figures as bold and stark in outline as the carved wooden figures on the cathedral rood-screen—figures representing a man and a woman side by side at the foot of the cross. Such a carving invites us to see not only the Mother of Jesus and the Beloved Disciple, as in the Fourth Gospel, but two human beings, one male and one female, coequal before God. We are invited to see them as partners in the way of the cross, which is the way of Christian transformation.

The text of Gen. 1:26–27 remains obscure, even after being

163

examined in all its manifold dimensions in order to discover what the image of God means. Whether Christians are human depends on their relationship with each other and with themselves and with the reality which lies beyond themselves—in the past and in the future, in this whole universe and beyond it. But one thing is certain. We walk the road of freedom together.

NOTES

1. F. J. Sheed, *Our Hearts are Restless: The Prayer of St. Augustine* (New York: Seabury Press, 1976), p. 76. The prayers which follow are in Sheed's translation from the same source.

2. F. Van Der Meer, *Augustine the Bishop,* Eng. trans. Brian Battershaw and G. R. Lamb (New York: Sheed and Ward, 1961), p. 176.

3. Ibid., p. 197.

4. Theophan the Recluse, as quoted by Henri J. M. Nouwen, *Reaching Out* (New York: Doubleday & Co., 1975), p. 88.

5. Charles Williams, ed., *The Letters of Evelyn Underhill* (London: Longmans, Green and Co., 1943), p. 37.

6. Lucy Menzies, ed., *Collected Papers of Evelyn Underhill* (London: Longmans, Green and Co., 1946), p. 55.

7. Ibid.

8. Ibid., p. 80.

9. Douglas Steere, *Prayer and Worship* (New York: Association Press, 1938), p. 11.

10. Simone Weil, *Waiting on God* (London: Routledge and Kegan Paul, 1951), p. 27.

11. Simone Weil, *First and Last Notebooks* (London: Oxford University Press, 1970), p. 99.

12. Weil, *Waiting on God,* p. 21.

13. Ibid., p. 139.

14. Nouwen, *Reaching Out,* p. 89.

15. Ibid., p. 95.

16. G. K. Chesterton, *St. Francis of Assisi* (New York: George H. Doran Co., 1924), p. 164.

17. Laurence Housman, *Little Plays of St. Francis,* Vol. II (London: Sidgwick & Jackson, 1935), p. 80.

18. E. Allison Peers, ed., *The Complete Works of Saint John of the Cross,* Vol. II (London: Burns, Oates and Washbourne, 1953), p. 4.

Index of
Proper Names

Post-Biblical